KINGDOM SECRETS TO
RESTORING NATIONS BACK TO GOD

DISCOVERING

THE LOST KINGDOM

DISCIPLING NATIONS SERIES #1
ABRAHAM JOHN

DISCOVERING THE LOST KINGDOM

Kingdom Secrets to Restoring Nations Back to God
Discipling Nations Series #1

Copyright © 2018 by Abraham John
Fifth Edition 2022
Published by Abraham John

www.TheKingdomNetwork.org
email: info@thekingdomnetwork.org
1-800-558-5020

ISBN: 979-8-312846-42-3
Published in the United States of America

All emphasis or additions within Scripture quotations are the author's own.

Unless otherwise indicated, all Scripture taken from the New King James Version®. Copyright © 1982 by Thomas Nelson. Used by permission. All rights reserved. Scriptures marked KJV are from the King James Version, which is in the public domain.

All rights reserved. No part of this book may be reproduced or transmitted in any form or by any means, electronic or mechanical, including photocopying, recording, or by any information storage and retrieval system, without permission in writing from the author.
Please direct your inquiries to mim@maximpact.org.

CONTENTS

Preface	5
Introduction	9
Chapter 1: 14 Reasons to Discover the Kingdom of God	17
Chapter 2: God's Eternal Purposes	37
Chapter 3: What is the Kingdom?	49
Chapter 4: The Creation and Fall of Man-Kind	65
Chapter 5: The Process of Salvation	79
Chapter 6: Why is the Message of the Kingdom so Vital	97
Chapter 7: Seek the Kingdom First	119
Chapter 8: The Most Liberating Message	139
Chapter 9: Eight Fundamental Needs of Every Human	159
Chapter 10: The Kingdom Prayer: Keys to Meeting All Our Needs	171
Chapter 11: Life in the Kingdom	187
Prayer	205

PREFACE

If God is love (which He is), then why do the majority of the people on earth not understand His love, or they struggle to receive it? If God is a good God (which He is), then why doesn't He answer the cry of everyone in need? Why is there so much suffering and pain in this world? Why do so many live in hunger and poverty?

These are the kinds of questions that turn many away from God and cause them to close their hearts off from Him. Even those who grew up in the church struggle with these questions at times. When life brings unexpected challenges, it's hard to find satisfying answers. We reject God and His plan for us because His ways and plans don't make any sense to our natural mind.

The difficulty in finding the answers to life's challenging questions lies in the failure to understand the purpose and plan of God. What was in His mind when He decided to create this planet and then put us on it?

When we understand His purpose and plan, then we will understand why things are happening the way they are. When we look at things from God's perspective, life and everything else around us will suddenly make perfect sense.

God never intended for anyone to live in poverty or experience hunger. He never intended for any evil on our planet. How do we justify and overcome pandemics like COVID-19 or other natural

DISCOVERING THE LOST KINGDOM

calamities? Illegal migration and refugee crises are in the news almost every day. Why do people from rich and developing countries try to escape from the country they were born into?

We've seen pictures from around the world of bodies washed ashore of those who tried to escape their countries. The sad truth is that many of them perish on their way; they couldn't reach their destination. What prompts people to risk their lives to embark on such a dangerous journey?

Whether you realize it yet or not, your heart has been searching for a lost kingdom. Until you find it, you will never really be happy on this earth. It doesn't matter who you are, what country you live in, how much wealth you possess, which religion you follow, or what type of church you have been attending—nothing will satisfy you or be an adequate substitute. You were created to live in and expand a kingdom. Religion wants us to believe that we are looking to go to heaven.

God didn't create mankind to live in heaven. Adam was not created to go to heaven, and he didn't lose heaven when he fell. God never mentioned anything to Adam about heaven. Adam was not created to die.

Death entered this planet as a result of sin. Sin entered because of the disobedience of man. What would we be doing on earth if Adam didn't sin and never fell?

God told Adam that the day he ate the fruit of the Tree of the Knowledge of Good and Evil, he would die. If he had not eaten from that tree, he would not have died spiritually or physically. If he hadn't died, he would be on the earth today doing what God told him to do in Genesis. Disobeying God's command, Adam ate from that tree. Spiritually, he died immediately, but physically, he died within the same day. For God, a thousand years on earth is one day, and no human has ever lived a thousand years on this earth *(2 Peter 3:8)*.

Jesus and the apostles never asked anyone if they wanted to go to heaven when they died. Just take a minute and think about that. If you die today, you will go to heaven to wait, but when the time comes, you will return to earth to rule and reign with Christ. Your purpose is always connected to planet Earth, in this life and in the next.

Why do I write about Rediscovering the Lost Kingdom? Originally, man was created and lived in the kingdom of God. We lost that kingdom because of disobedience. God is merciful and decided to restore it to us because He knows we can't function without it, and that we will keep searching until we find it. That's why He sent Jesus with the message of the kingdom.

All trouble on this earth began as the result of mankind losing God's kingdom. Poverty, hunger, racism, failed governments, different religions, denominations, and every type of evil are the results that stemmed from that one event in human history.

If we don't find it, we will substitute it with destructive things. People have been trying to replace it with pleasant activities, entertainment, education, religion, sex, music, luxury, money, fame, and many other avenues—but none of those pursuits pay off. They all leave us empty and unfulfilled inside.

> ***I must preach the kingdom of God to the other cities also,***
> ***because for this purpose I have been sent. (Luke 4:43)***

This statement is Jesus's own words. He was saying that He was sent to preach the kingdom of God. Why did He come preaching the kingdom? What do we have to do with it? Why was the kingdom

DISCOVERING THE LOST KINGDOM

of God the most important subject God had to communicate with mankind? Why did God have to send His only begotten Son to tell us about it?

This book is designed to fulfill the age-old search of every human heart for a lost country in which righteousness, peace, and joy are the center of its culture. In God's kingdom, you will experience peace in spite of what is happening around you.

God sent Jesus with a kingdom message because He knew His kingdom is the permanent solution for hunger, death, racism, poverty, unemployment, religious conflict, and every type of evil we see on planet Earth.

This is only an introduction to the journey of rediscovering that lost kingdom. I encourage you to read it slowly and study it until it changes the way you think and function, until a kingdom mindset is formed in you. At the end of this book, you will find information for what to do next.

I can guarantee this will be the most exciting and fulfilling journey you ever take in your lifetime. Many righteous men and kings desired to see what you are about to see and read, but they did not get the opportunity (Matthew 13:17). In that sense, you are very special and privileged. Welcome to the journey of rediscovering the lost kingdom!

INTRODUCTION

The word of the day is kingdom. Believers everywhere are talking about the kingdom of God; kingdom age and kingdom move are being discussed more than ever before. Theologians and church leaders have come up with various teachings about it: "Kingdom now, but not yet" theology, dominionism, dispensationalism, denominationalism, and the anticipation of an imminent rapture have distorted the understanding of it for a long time.

What was in the mind of God when He decided to create the earth and humans?

Did He want to listen from heaven to a bunch of people singing and playing music every Sunday morning? Did He want to have a family and keep them separated from Him on a faraway planet? Did He create the earth as a breeding place to populate heaven? We are His family in His kingdom, but why did He put us here and not keep us with Him in heaven? Did He have something greater in mind?

Our God is a King forever and ever *(Psalm 10:16; 1 Timothy 1:17)*. He is not just a King; He is the King of all kings. He has a kingdom, which is the kingdom of heaven. When you think of heaven, try to think of it as a kingdom rather than a floating cloudy place somewhere up in the sky with angels singing.

The very reason God created our planet was to extend His kingdom. God entrusted us with accomplishing that task. Instead, we have been debating, arguing, and rebelling against it for thousands of years.

Just because we add the word kingdom to our already-existing religious vocabulary doesn't mean we become people of the kingdom. Many others, because of misunderstanding and the fear of being labeled a heretic, threw the kingdom message out with the bathwater. They were nervous about teaching this subject and afraid of being in error. Most of them hid the message for fear of people or to appease men.

Keep in mind that the message of the kingdom is the most important subject in the Bible—and was the most frequent message Jesus preached while He was on the earth with the apostles in the first-century church. If preaching the kingdom was important for Jesus and His apostles, it should be important for us, too.

People often ask me whether or not the apostle Paul preached about the kingdom or mentioned the gospel of the kingdom. They think he only preached about grace. In Acts alone, there are at least five instances where Paul preached about the kingdom of God; it was the most important subject he preached during his missionary journeys *(Acts 14:21-22, 19:8, 20:25, 28:23, 28:30-31)*.

Many think the church age needs to come to an end so the kingdom age can begin. That's not true. The kingdom and the church are supposed to function simultaneously. One won't work without the other. It is a misconception that the church is waiting for the rapture to take place so the kingdom age can manifest.

WHAT IS THE KINGDOM AGE?

People sometimes get confused when they hear terms like *kingdom age, church age, and millennial reign*. The kingdom age refers to the time period in which God decided to rule this planet with His kingdom. That means the kingdom age began the moment God's rule began on this planet, in relation to mankind in Genesis 1. His kingdom is an everlasting kingdom and His dominion endures from generation to generation *(Psalm 145:13; Daniel 4:3, 34)*.

The kingdom and the church are not the same. The kingdom of God includes everything God ever created.

There's no way to measure the size or the vastness of it. The church has been operating without the kingdom for a long time. That is why it is powerless and irrelevant to society—and unable to solve the problems we face in the world today. A church without the kingdom of God is powerless. A kingdom without a church or ekklesia is useless. The church is the governing body of the kingdom. Jesus never intended for His church to operate apart from His kingdom.

It's impossible to separate a king from his kingdom. If you do so, neither of them will survive. Jesus and His kingdom are one, and they are inseparable. A church without the kingdom will not survive or will be lifeless, as a body without a spirit is dead.

We told people to come to Jesus but did not teach them how to live in His kingdom. Though they received Jesus, many remain in hunger, sickness, and hopelessness because they did not hear the whole gospel. We separated Jesus from His kingdom.

The church, or ekklesia, has been in existence as long as the kingdom of God has been in existence. If you want to know more about this subject, please read the book *The Ekklesia: Purpose, Power, and Function*. God created man to establish and manage His kingdom on earth, but we have done everything on earth except that. We have deviated from our purpose for a long time. At last, God is bringing us back to our original intent, and bringing the message

DISCOVERING THE LOST KINGDOM

of the kingdom back to His church so the church can become powerful once again.

The church is supposed to be the epicenter of everything that happens in a community and nation. It is supposed to be the resource center for the natural, spiritual, and social needs of people. It was never meant to be an icon or monument on a street corner. It was never meant to be a religious business center or a building in which people gather on a Sunday morning. It's supposed to be the lifeline and lighthouse for those who are lost; the place people should run to find God and the solutions to their problems. It was meant to be the visible manifestation of the invisible kingdom of God on earth.

The church is supposed to be the training ground where we equip believers to discover and fulfill their kingdom assignment on earth. It was never supposed to be a place that prepared people to live in heaven. No training is needed to live in heaven.

The devil knows that if he can distort and take the kingdom message away from God's people, they will not be any threat to his kingdom on this earth. He has succeeded and hidden that message from us for too long.

The Bible is not a religious book. It's a book about a King, His government, His royal family, and the plan He has for the earth. His plan from the beginning has been to establish His kingdom on earth. But that plan has been delayed because the very people He appointed to carry it out rebelled and didn't cooperate with Him. He will not change His mind or plan about it, no matter what happens.

I want you to remove any theological misunderstanding you may have in your heart that says God does not want to see His kingdom come to the earth now. He hasn't put it away for some time in the future or changed His mind about it. He never did and never will. Otherwise, Jesus wouldn't have told us to pray for His kingdom to come. What He purposed before eternity will come to pass—and nothing and no one can change it.

Our life here on earth is not a mistake; it did not begin because of the fall of Adam, and it is not the result of a sin or curse. Our life is God's original idea and design. Each day we get to spend here is a great privilege and honor. *Living in God's kingdom is the greatest thing a human being gets to do!* The sooner we align with God's kingdom agenda, the sooner our life on earth will get better and become more meaningful. Until then, life will feel like it is torture and an inconvenience.

Another misunderstanding some have is that God will establish His kingdom on earth, but not on this earth as we know it now. They believe it will be on the new earth. As long as you have that theological disposition, the enemy has won his battle against you, because your future and the future of your nation will look grim. You will simply be waiting to leave this planet.

Everyone God chose in the Bible was used to establish His kingdom and will on earth as it is in heaven, and the very reason He put you on this earth is to accomplish that! What would have happened (to us and the earth) if the people in Bible times believed like we believe and lived like we do?

God never took a break, and there was never a time in the history of mankind when He told us to take a break from His purpose. As long as God exists, His kingdom will exist and its rule will continue on earth and in the entire universe. As much as man cooperates with Him, the manifestation of it in the natural will vary from place to place and age to age.

DISCOVERING THE LOST KINGDOM

Your kingdom is an everlasting kingdom, and Your dominion endures throughout all generations. (Psalm 145:13)

For His dominion is an everlasting dominion, and His kingdom is from generation to generation. (Daniel 4:34b)

But the Lord is the true God; He is the living God and the everlasting King. (Jeremiah 10:10a)

His kingdom is an everlasting kingdom, and all dominions shall serve and obey Him. (Daniel 7:27b)

Your throne, O God, is forever and ever; a scepter of righteousness is the scepter of Your kingdom. (Hebrews 1:8)

The verses above clearly tell us that God's kingdom is everlasting and that His dominion endures throughout all generations. I encourage you to believe the Bible over the opinion of any theologian or teacher out there. There was a heathen king who had a better understanding and grasp of God and His kingdom than most of our church theologians. It was Nebuchadnezzar, who spoke the above verse in Daniel 4. Please refer to the following verses for further proof: 1 Peter 4:11, 5:11; Jude 1:25; Revelation 1:6. I also believe the fullness of the physical manifestation of the kingdom of God will only happen when Christ returns. Until then, we will only have partial understanding and manifestation of it in different places on earth.

My purpose for writing these revelations about the kingdom of God is not to establish a physical kingdom with thrones and palaces. We don't take over cities, nations, or governments. That is not the way the kingdom of God operates now. The purpose of this book is to open the eyes of believers to the message of the kingdom, to equip the body of Christ to disciple nations with the gospel of the kingdom, and to train believers to live in and manifest the kingdom based on their specific calling and spiritual maturity.

When Christ returns, there will be sheep and goat nations on the earth. As far as I know, there is not a nation on earth today that serves Him. The gospel of salvation will bring souls into the kingdom, but only the gospel of the kingdom has power to save nations. We are entering a new era and season where the message of the kingdom will be preached as never before. The whole world is waiting for it!

> ***The law and the prophets were until John. Since that time the kingdom of God has been preached, and everyone is pressing into it. (Luke 16:16)***

When we preach what Jesus and the apostles preached, souls will press in to enter the kingdom of God. We don't need to coerce them with fake miracles or material prosperity nor threaten them with hell. Every soul is longing for the kingdom. Welcome to the journey.

CHAPTER 1
14 REASONS TO DISCOVER THE KINGDOM OF GOD

The law and the prophets were until John. Since that time the kingdom of God has been preached, and everyone is pressing into it. (Luke 16:16)

Why discovering the lost kingdom? Jesus told us to seek His kingdom first. If we already have something in our possession, then we don't need to seek it; we seek something we lost or can't find. The reason Jesus told us to seek His kingdom is because we lost it. Below are the fourteen reasons we need to study and discover the kingdom of God.

1. IT IS THE MOST IMPORTANT SUBJECT IN THE BIBLE

The entire Bible is about a King, His kingdom, His royal family, and His plan for planet Earth. Each verse in the Bible talks about one of the things mentioned above. Either they are about our King, His kingdom, or His royal family—which is us—or about what He would like to see happen on this planet *(Psalm 10:16; 22:28; 1 Timothy 1:17)*.

When you read the Bible from the above-mentioned perspective, you will receive much more from it. There are human errors in the Bible caused by various translations and misinterpretations, but the revelation of God in the Bible is inerrant, intact, and steady from Genesis to Revelation.

So many ministers discredit the Bible by pointing out the human errors in it. These people have not come to the knowledge of the truth yet. They do not understand who God is and His purpose for mankind and this planet. I wonder how they even became ministers in the first place.

2. JESUS COMMANDED US TO SEEK IT FIRST

Why would our Lord, our King, and the Owner of this universe tell mankind to seek His kingdom first? When God says we need to do something first, He means it. Unfortunately, we misunderstood what He meant. Most people have interpreted Jesus's command to mean getting baptized first or becoming a member of a particular type of church first. Or maybe they thought He was saying that we should go out and witness or do some kind of ministry for Him first. But that is not what He meant at all. Those are the various interpretations caused by the influence of the religious spirit *(Matthew 6:33)*.

One of the main reasons for this book is to find out what Jesus really meant by telling us to seek His kingdom first. By the end of this book, you will have good understanding of why He told us that and how to walk it out. May the Holy Spirit help each one of us understand the heart of our King.

3. IT IS GOD'S PRIORITY

The third reason we need to discover the kingdom of God is because it is God's priority. Whatever He does, He does it with one intent in mind. He wants to see His kingdom expand to new territories. Whatever God does in relation to this earth, He does it to see His kingdom come and His will established here as it is in heaven. He wants to colonize the earth with His kingdom. He wants the earth to be a reflection of heaven *(Matthew 6:9-10; John 3:3; Luke 9:59-60)*.

When we understand the reason God does something, then we can know Him and His ways. Whether He saves, heals, restores, builds, creates, or delivers, the end result of all those actions is to see His kingdom dream become real in another individual and to another part of the earth.

4. IT IS THE SUBJECT THAT JESUS TAUGHT THE MOST WHILE HE WAS ON EARTH

From the first day of His ministry until His last day on earth, Jesus had only one subject to teach to humanity— and that was all about His kingdom (Matthew 4:17; Acts 1:3). His message was not about us going to heaven; His message was about His kingdom coming to earth.

Jesus healed people, but healing was not His message. He delivered people, but deliverance was not His message. He was full of grace, but grace was not His message. Day in and day out, His message was centered on the kingdom of heaven and the kingdom of God.

There is a reason Jesus preached about the kingdom more than any other subject. He was not trying to save everyone He met. He was focused on His mission and the purpose for which His Father sent Him to earth *(Luke 4:43)*.

5. THE KINGDOM IS WHY GOD CREATED THE EARTH AND PUT MANKIND ON IT

God is King. It is the glory and the nature of kings to expand their kingdom to new territories. God decided to expand His kingdom to a new territory called planet Earth. That is the reason He created the earth *(Psalm 103:19; Matthew 6:9-10; Revelation 11:15)*.

6. OUR PURPOSE IS CONNECTED TO GOD'S KINGDOM

God created this earth to establish His kingdom. He wanted someone to manage that venture and the earth. That's why He created us. We were created for the earth and for the kingdom and for the glory of God. If there's no kingdom of God, then there's no reason for us to be here. We are not the center of the universe; Jesus and His kingdom are the center of the universe. We were created to take care of the earth. Earth was not created for us; we were created for the earth *(Genesis 1:26; 2:19; Matthew 16:19)*

7. OUR PROVISION IS CONNECTED TO GOD'S KINGDOM

Our God is the most benevolent King in this universe. We were created for His kingdom purpose, so when someone commits to fulfill their God-given kingdom assignment, God then makes an eternal promise to provide, protect, and take care of that person. That's one of the reasons He told us to seek His kingdom first *(Matthew 6:33)*. He knows we are worried about our livelihood.

If someone is going hungry on this planet, it is because they are ignorant of God's kingdom and their assignment in it. God will go to any length to protect and take care of a kingdom citizen. People who live outside of His kingdom or are not carrying out their kingdom assignment are on their own to provide for and protect themselves *(Genesis 2:8; 15,16)*.

That's the reason God doesn't answer the cry of everyone who is in need. He is committed to His kingdom and its citizens. Someone can be a member of a church and not live in God's kingdom or be aware of it.

Others can even be doing ministry and still miss their kingdom assignment. This might sound shocking, but we will learn more about this later in this book. How did the Pharisees miss Jesus and His kingdom when they thought they were living for God and were the most spiritual and holy people on earth? It is quite possible, and it is scary.

8. THE KINGDOM OF GOD IS THE SOLUTION FOR EVERY PROBLEM ON THE EARTH

God never intended for the earth to function without His kingdom.

The earth was created to be an extension of God's kingdom—and it cannot properly function without it. When the kingdom of God is absent from an area or sphere of life, we will have problems. When the kingdom of God is absent from the land, then the land won't produce like it should. When it is absent from the government, we will have political instability.

When the kingdom of God is absent from the family, then family life won't work the way it should. When the kingdom of God is absent from the education system, people will be taught ungodly things.

It's the same with the church. When the kingdom of God is absent from the church, it will become a religion or social club; the church will cease to be effective. That's why we have so many people who are sick and poor in churches all over the world. The early church had five thousand people, and nobody in the entire church had an unmet need or was sick in their body (*Matthew 9:35; Luke 4:43; 8:1; 9:1-2*).

There may be times when we think that we have lost the Holy Spirit, but we didn't lose the Holy Spirit, He was sent to live in us and with us forever. What we lost is the kingdom of God or the revelation of it. The Holy Spirit was sent to manifest the kingdom through us. When we neglect the kingdom of God and try to build our own little kingdoms or ministries, then the Holy Spirit stops manifesting. When we turn from our wicked ways and acknowledge the purpose for which God sent us to this planet, and partner with Him to accomplish His will, then we will see the manifestation of the Holy Spirit again in our churches.

9. OUR TIME, SKILL, AND STRENGTH ARE SUPPOSED TO BE USED TO BUILD THE KINGDOM OF GOD

The greatest commandment in the Bible is to love our God with all our heart, soul, mind, and strength *(Mark 12:30)*. That means with everything we have and everything we are; we are supposed to be using these to love Him; not just ten percent or for two hours on a Sunday morning.

Every skill that we possess, all of our time here on earth, and the strength that God has given to every individual, is supposed to be used to build His kingdom and to establish His will on earth as it is in heaven. We were sent here to fulfill a specific assignment for His kingdom. That assignment will require every ounce of our energy, skill, and time. At the same time, people's hearts are empty, and they are trying to fill the void with the things of the world.

When we begin to fulfill our kingdom purpose, we will find great joy and peace, and all the things we need will be added to us. *(Matthew 6:33)*

Right now, most believers are not serving God and His kingdom with the majority of their time and skills; instead, they are trying to make a living serving another kingdom. This has been happening mainly because of ignorance and should not be so. As the Bible says, God's people are destroyed for lack of knowledge:

> **The law and the prophets were until John. Since that time the kingdom of God has been preached, and everyone is pressing into it. (Luke 16:16)**

10. THE EARTH WAS CREATED TO BE AN EXTENSION OF GOD'S KINGDOM

God wants the same quality of life, culture, economy, and way of living that is in the heavenly realms to manifest on the earth. That is what is meant by "on earth as it is in heaven." He never intended for life on earth to be any different than life in heaven. The life we are dreaming about living in heaven, He wants us to live right now on earth *(Matthew 6:10)*.

The kingdom of God is the source, and earth is supposed to be an extension of it. We got disconnected from our source. It is like launching a spaceship. If the spaceship loses the connection with its base or control tower on earth, then it gets lost and misses the whole purpose for which it was launched.

Mankind declared independence from God and His kingdom by entering into an allegiance with an enemy kingdom. When mankind renounces their allegiance to the enemy kingdom and declares their dependence on God and His kingdom, life and earth will begin to change for the better.

11. WE CAN'T LIVE WITHOUT A KINGDOM

We are kingdom builders by design because we are created in the image and likeness of God. He is a kingdom builder *(Luke 12:32; Colossians 1:11)*. As I mentioned earlier, whatever He does, He does it for the progress of His kingdom. Whatever we do from the time we wake until the time we go to sleep, we are building kingdoms.

The question is: Whose kingdom are we building?

We are either building God's kingdom, the enemy's kingdom, or our own little kingdom. We were created to live in a kingdom. No other form of government will work for us except God's government. It is our choice to live in and build His kingdom, or not.

12. WITHOUT UNDERSTANDING THE KINGDOM WE WON'T UNDERSTAND THE PURPOSE AND FUNCTION OF THE CHURCH

Have you ever wondered why the church is in such a big mess? We are fragmented into millions of groups and names because we are functioning outside of God's kingdom. That is why Jesus spent more than three years teaching and training the disciples about the kingdom of God before He introduced or mentioned anything about the church. He knew that without having an understanding of His kingdom, they wouldn't understand the church and its purpose *(Matthew 16:18)*.

Most of us won't hear much about God's kingdom. All we hear about is the church and about going to heaven when we die. In the early apostles' case, the first and the last thing they heard from Jesus was all about His kingdom. So when the church was birthed, they looked at it from a kingdom perspective. In our case, when we hear about the kingdom, we try to look at it from a church perspective— and we miss the entire thing!

Without the kingdom, we won't understand the purpose of the church. Without the kingdom, the church will end up as a religion or little kingdoms of so-called ministers. It's time for the worldwide body of Christ to go back to our roots—kingdom roots.

13. ALL WEALTH AND RESOURCES THAT GOD PUT ON EARTH MUST BE USED TO BUILD HIS KINGDOM

Every resource God created on the earth is supposed to be used to build His kingdom and to accomplish His will on earth as it is in heaven. He did not create anything for the devil, nor did the devil create anything. Unfortunately, the majority of the wealth and resources on the earth are being used by the enemy and his children to build his evil kingdom. This must stop!

This will only happen when the sons and daughters of God rise up and take their place in the nations of the world and fulfill their kingdom assignments *(Haggai 2:8; Joel 3:5)*.

14. THE KINGDOM IS THE SUBJECT THE APOSTLE PAUL AND OTHERS PREACHED

When the Father sent His Son to earth, the only message He was authorized to preach and teach humans were the message of the kingdom *(Luke 4:43)*. When Jesus sent His disciples or apostles to preach, the only message He authorized them to preach was the message of the kingdom *(Matthew 10:7; Luke 9:1)*. We are going to see how Jesus and the apostles preached the message of the kingdom in the following lines.

JESUS AND THE APOSTLES PRREACHED THE KINGDOM

When I share or preach about the gospel of the kingdom, many people are skeptical. They ask various questions like: Did Paul or Peter preach about the kingdom of God? They think that only Jesus preached about the kingdom, and the apostles preached about grace or going to heaven. Following are some of the evidences from Scripture that show that both Jesus and the apostles preached the kingdom of God.

JESUS PREACHED THE KINGDOM OF GOD

Jesus began His earthly ministry by declaring the arrival of the kingdom in Matthew 4:17, and He ended it after His resurrection when He spoke to them about the kingdom of God again in Acts 1:3. He did not preach healing; He preached the kingdom and then healed the sick. He did not preach deliverance; He preached the kingdom and delivered people. He did not preach prosperity; He came with the gospel of the kingdom. There is prosperity in His kingdom.

> ***Then Jesus went about all the cities and villages, teaching in their synagogues, preaching the gospel of the kingdom, and healing every sickness and every disease among the people. (Matthew 9:35)***
>
> ***Now after John was put in prison, Jesus came to Galilee, preaching the gospel of the kingdom of God. (Mark 1:14)***
>
> ***But He said to them, "I must preach the kingdom of God to the other cities also, because for this purpose I have been sent." (Luke 4:43)***

14 REASONS TO DISCOVER THE KINGDOM OF GOD

There are several schools of thought about the kingdom of God among today's Christians and theologians. Many of them are not biblical.

One school of thought says that Jesus preached the kingdom because that is what the Jewish people were waiting for: the liberation of Israel from the rule of Rome, to reestablish them as a kingdom. So to suffice their expectation and to make them happy, Jesus preached the kingdom for three and a half years and no one preached the kingdom after Jesus died. In other words, Jesus was beguiling them by talking about the kingdom, which He was not planning to establish anyway at that time.

The second school of thought says that Jesus came to give the kingdom to Israel but they rejected it, so God postponed it and inserted a parenthetical church age that had not originally been planned. After the church is raptured, the gospel of the kingdom will again be preached (by the Jewish people) during the great tribulation. Both of these are philosophies created academically and are not supported by Scripture.

Jesus came to give them a kingdom, which He stated very plainly in Luke 12:32:

> **Then Jesus went about all the cities and villages, teaching in their synagogues, preaching the gospel of the kingdom, and healing every sickness and every disease among the people (Matthew 9:35).**

They did not reject the kingdom; they rejected Jesus. They did not want Him to be their king because He did not fit their idea of how a king would act and live. So Jesus told them He would take the kingdom from them and give it to another nation.

DISCOVERING THE LOST KINGDOM

Jesus said to them, "Have you never read in the Scriptures: 'The stone which the builders rejected has become the chief cornerstone. This was the Lord's doing, and it is marvelous in our eyes'? Therefore I say to you, the kingdom of God will be taken from you and given to a nation bearing the fruits of it." *(Matthew 21:42–43)*

The nation to which Jesus refers in this verse is the church. We are called a holy nation in 1 Peter 2:9. The Jewish people were expecting the arrival of their Messiah to restore their kingdom. That part is true. But the type of kingdom God was planning to establish through Jesus at His first coming was not an earthly or physical kingdom, but spiritual. So they rejected Him. The Jewish people did not reject the kingdom. They were waiting and asking for it.

Even after the resurrection the disciples asked Jesus about this.

> **Therefore, when they had come together, they asked Him, saying, "Lord, will You at this time restore the kingdom to Israel?" (Acts 1:6)**

They were still expecting a natural kingdom. In another place we read:

> **Now as they heard these things, He spoke another parable, because He was near Jerusalem and because they thought the kingdom of God would appear immediately. (Luke 19:11)**

The parable Jesus shared was about a nobleman going away to a far country to receive for himself a kingdom and then return. He called his servants and gave them his goods to do business until he returned *(Luke 19:12–27)*. That parable is applicable to us today. It is what we are supposed to be doing while we wait for the return of our King.

14 REASONS TO DISCOVER THE KINGDOM OF GOD

The kingdom appeared on the day of Pentecost, and it was a spiritual kingdom. When we study the book of Acts, we see that the apostles preached the kingdom of God, especially to the gentiles. After the arrival of the Holy Spirit, only the disciples understood what kind of kingdom Jesus had been preaching about all those years.

JESUS PREACHED THE KINGDOM OF GOD AFTER HIS RESURRECTION

> ***To whom He also presented Himself alive after His suffering by many infallible proofs, being seen by them during forty days and speaking of the things pertaining to the kingdom of God. (Acts 1:3)***

PETER PREACHED THE KINGDOM OF GOD

What I did not understand for a long time was the message Peter preached on the day of Pentecost. I wondered why he did not mention anything about the kingdom of God in his message. Why was it only about repentance and baptism? I was ignorant and blinded by the religious spirit for a long time, and that is why I did not see anything about God's kingdom in his message.

To be honest, Peter spoke about repentance and baptism only after people asked him what they should do, after they heard his preaching. The theme of the message he preached prior to that was about David and his throne, and how God raised Jesus to sit on that throne. He preached the kingdom of God from a historical perspective and showed that Jesus is the fulfillment of the prophecies and promises God gave to David.

Peter preached more about the kingdom of God (without using the word kingdom) in that one message than anyone else in the entire book of Acts. He referred to David and his throne several times. What does David have to do with the day of Pentecost? Or the arrival of the Holy Spirit? Or the inauguration of the church? Why would Peter refer to David in the first message ever preached in the Church Age? This gets very interesting. There are ten references to David and nine references to Abraham in the book of Acts.

David was a special man. He is the first individual in the Bible who received the revelation that God is King and has a kingdom, and wrote about it. He wrote about it throughout his psalms. God was ecstatic about this because He is King forever and ever. He has a kingdom that He wants to establish on the earth. When He found out there was at least one man who understood His purpose and heart, He couldn't have been happier.

God is King and has the heart of a king. That is why He said David was a man after His own heart. David was a king. The religious spirit taught us that God referred that way about David because of his singing and dancing.

There were many skilled musicians and singers during David's time, but God did not tell to any one of them that they were people after His own heart or make any special covenant with them. He only said that to David because of his revelation of who God is and about His kingdom.

Because of the revelation David had of God's kingdom, God made an eternal covenant with him and his house, saying his kingdom and his throne would endure forever. The resurrection of Jesus was the fulfillment of that covenant and promise God made with David. Jesus is the Son of David and the legal heir to David's throne. When the Holy Spirit gave Peter this revelation, he preached about it on the day of Pentecost. He was preaching to a crowd of people that were mainly Jewish (*2 Samuel 7:12-16; Luke 1:31-33*).

> *When your days are fulfilled and you rest with your fathers, I will set up your seed after you, who will come from your body, and I will establish his kingdom. He shall build a house for My name, and I will establish the throne of his kingdom forever. I will be his Father, and he shall be My son. If he commits iniquity, I will chasten him with the rod of men and with the blows of the sons of men. But My mercy shall not depart from him, as I took it from Saul, whom I removed from before you. And your house and your kingdom shall be established forever before you. Your throne shall be established forever. (2 Samuel 7:12-16)*

Jesus was called the Son of David throughout the gospels. The Holy Spirit gave Peter a revelation about that when He stood up to preach. It had everything to do with God's eternal kingdom plan for planet Earth.

> *Men and brethren, let me speak freely to you of the patriarch David, that he is both dead and buried, and his tomb is with us to this day. Therefore, being a prophet, and knowing that God had sworn with an oath to him that of the fruit of his body, according to the flesh, He would raise up the Christ to sit on his throne, he, foreseeing this, spoke concerning the resurrection of the Christ, that His soul was not left in Hades, nor did His flesh see corruption. This Jesus God has raised up, of which we are all witnesses. Therefore, being exalted to the right hand of God, and having received from the Father the promise of the Holy Spirit, He poured out this which you now see and hear. For David did not ascend into the heavens, but he says himself:*

> *"The Lord said to my Lord,*
> *'Sit at My right hand,*
> *Till I make Your enemies Your footstool.'" (Acts 2:29–35)*

When those Jewish people heard that message, they understood it and were cut to the heart and ran to him. Jesus said that from the day of John the Baptist, the kingdom of God was being preached and everyone was pressing into it. Three thousand people ran to Peter to get into the kingdom that day.

It is Interesting to look at how each of the gospels presents the entry of Jesus into Jerusalem. When the people shouted, "Hosanna in the highest!" or "Hosanna!" to the Son of David, Mark recorded it with David's kingdom, which we do not see in the other gospels.

> *Then those who went before and those who followed cried out, saying:*
> *"Hosanna!*
> *'Blessed is He who comes in the name of the Lord!'*
> *Blessed is the kingdom of our father David that comes in the name of the Lord! Hosanna in the highest!"*
> *(Mark 11:9–10)*

In His triumphal or royal entry into Jerusalem, He was fulfilling one of the major prophecies in the Old Testament because He actually was their King.

> *Rejoice greatly, O daughter of Zion! Shout, O daughter of Jerusalem! Behold, your King is coming to you; He is just and having salvation, Lowly and riding on a donkey, A colt, the foal of a donkey. (Zechariah 9:9)*

Clearly, God did not "insert" the church into His original plan; the church had been His plan all along.

14 REASONS TO DISCOVER THE KINGDOM OF GOD

PHILIP PREACHED THE KINGDOM OF GOD TO THE PEOPLE OF SAMARIA

> *But when they believed Philip as he preached the things concerning the kingdom of God and the name of Jesus Christ, both men and women were baptized. (Acts 8:12)*

JOHN PREACHED THE KINGDOM OF GOD

> *Jesus answered and said to him, "Most assuredly, I say to you, unless one is born again, he cannot see the kingdom of God." (John 3:3)*

> *I, John, both your brother and companion in the tribulation and kingdom and patience of Jesus Christ, was on the island that is called Patmos for the word of God and for the testimony of Jesus Christ. (Revelation 1:9)*

> *Then the seventh angel sounded: And there were loud voices in heaven, saying,*

> *"The kingdoms of this world have become the kingdoms of our Lord and of His Christ, and He shall reign forever and ever!" (Revelation 11:15)*

The above verse in Revelation is one of my favorite verses concerning the kingdom of God and the future of the earth. People ask if I am concerned about the antichrist, mark of the beast, one world government, or tribulation. I tell them that I am not focused on the antichrist and what the devil is doing on the earth. One thing I know is that sooner or later, the kingdoms of this world will become the kingdoms of our Lord and of His Christ, and He shall reign forever and ever. That is my focus, the reason for my existence, and my future.

DISCOVERING THE LOST KINGDOM

When there are that many references to the apostles preaching the kingdom of God, it is difficult to understand why so-called theologians and preachers today have a problem approving the message of the kingdom. It has always been the religious system and the religious spirit that opposes the message of the kingdom of God.

When you see someone who does not like the message of the kingdom, it is clear evidence that a religious spirit is operating in that person. When Jesus was here on earth, the gentiles and sinners did not oppose Him or what He preached. It was the religious leaders who opposed Him and did not like what He preached. Some things have not changed.

PAUL PREACHED THE KINGDOM OF GOD AND SPOKE ABOUT ENTERING IT

Many people ask me about whether or not Paul preached the kingdom. Yes—of course! It was the only message he preached and taught during his missionary journeys. If you are truly saved and called, especially to the office of an apostle, you have to preach the kingdom. If someone claims to be an apostle and doesn't have a revelation of the kingdom of God, he is likely not a true apostle or is immature.

There's no other subject on this planet or in the Bible that is as important as the kingdom. Below are the verses that show that Paul preached the kingdom of God:

In Lystra, Iconium, and Antioch:

> ***Strengthening the souls of the disciples, exhorting them to continue in the faith, and saying, "We must through many tribulations enter the kingdom of God." (Acts 14:22)***

14 REASONS TO DISCOVER THE KINGDOM OF GOD

In Ephesus:

And he went into the synagogue and spoke boldly for three months, reasoning and persuading concerning the things of the kingdom of God. (Acts 19:8)

Elders meeting in Ephesus:

And indeed, now I know that you all, among whom I have gone preaching the kingdom of God, will see my face no more. (Acts 20:25)

In Rome:

So when they had appointed him a day, many came to him at his lodging, to whom he explained and solemnly testified of the kingdom of God, persuading them concerning Jesus from both the Law of Moses and the Prophets, from morning till evening. (Acts 28:23)

Then Paul dwelt two whole years in his own rented house, and received all who came to him, preaching the kingdom of God and teaching the things which concern the Lord Jesus Christ with all confidence, no one forbidding him. (Acts 28:30–31)

Paul was an apostle called to the gentiles. This debunks the idea that says the message of the kingdom is only for the Jewish people during the Great Tribulation. The gospel of the kingdom is for the whole world and for the entire human race in every generation.

You may wonder why we don't see as many references to the kingdom in the Epistles that Paul and others wrote as we see in the Gospels. The Gospels were written to reveal the *message* of the

DISCOVERING THE LOST KINGDOM

kingdom. The Epistles were written to deal with *life* in the kingdom. One deals with the message, and the other deals with the challenges and questions that arise when we start living a kingdom life.

CHAPTER 2
GOD'S ETERNAL PURPOSES

The Lord is King forever and ever. (Psalm 10:16a)

Before we venture out to do anything in life, we first need to understand God's purpose and design because He always starts everything with purpose. Why does He do what He does, and how does He do it? Once we understand this, life becomes easy and meaningful. Purpose gives us the end picture. Design gives us the procedure (or the process) to accomplish the purpose; it is the blueprint. When you have the end picture of something, then you can understand where things fit, why things are happening the way they are, and where and how everything is going to conclude.

Everything God does is based on His purpose and design. God has seven eternal purposes in relation to earth and mankind. In this book, we will only touch on three of them. Our entire life is based on these three purposes. The first one is this:

1. GOD IS KING HE HAS A KINGDOM THAT HE WANTS TO SEE ESTABLISHED ON THE EARTH THAT IS HIS ULTIMATE PURPOSE AND PLAN

This is the reason behind everything God has been doing from the beginning of time in relation to earth. Whether He creates, heals, saves, or delivers, He does everything with one Big Picture in mind. He wants to see His kingdom come to this planet. Every other doctrine in the Bible should fit under this one; otherwise, we will end up in error or some form of religious extremism.

> *Now to the King eternal, immortal, invisible, to God who alone is wise, be honor and glory forever and ever. Amen. (1 Timothy 1:17)*
>
> *The Lord is King forever and ever. (Psalm 10:16a)*
>
> *Yours, O Lord, is the greatness, the power and the glory, the victory and the majesty; for all that is in heaven and in earth is Yours; yours is the kingdom, O Lord, and You are exalted as head over all. (1 Chronicles 29:11)*
>
> *The Lord has established His throne in heaven, and His kingdom rules over all. (Psalm 103:19) Your kingdom is an everlasting kingdom, and Your dominion endures throughout all generations. (Psalm 145:12)*
>
> *For the kingdom is the Lord's, and He rules over the nations. (Psalm 22:28)*
>
> *In this manner, therefore, pray: Our Father in heaven, hallowed be Your name. Your kingdom come. Your will be done on earth as it is in heaven. (Matthew 6:9–10)*

Then the seventh angel sounded: And there were loud voices in heaven, saying, "The kingdoms of this world have become the kingdoms of our Lord and of His Christ, and He shall reign forever and ever!" (Revelation 11:15)

These verses and many more like them show that God's plan has remained the same throughout all generations. He doesn't have any new plans for the earth or mankind. When we align ourselves with God's eternal purpose, life becomes meaningful. The church today doesn't operate within the above mentioned purpose. That's why we are powerless and irrelevant to society.

This is why so many people have difficulty understanding and relating to God. When He speaks or does something, He does it within the context of His eternal plan. We will find His love and ways of operation only within the limits of His purpose.

To fulfill this purpose, God created a species in His image and likeness called humans. Our assignment has always been to see God's purpose for the earth fulfilled. This leads us to God's second eternal purpose:

2. GOD WANTS MANKIND TO RULE AND REIGN ON EARTH WITH HIM AND ON HIS BEHALF

Adamah: Land or Ground

The name of the first human God created was *Adam*. The name *Adam* means "mankind," and it is taken from the Hebrew word *adamah*[1], which means "land" or "ground." By taking our body from the ground, God revealed a clue about our purpose.

---

[1] James Strong, "127. Adamah," Strong's Hebrew: 127. אדמה (adamah) -- ground, land (Biblehub), accessed May 12, 2020, https://biblehub.com/hebrew/127.htm)

Adam was not the name of an individual, but the name of a species, like monkey, fish, or lion.

Adam means "man of the land or earth." We were created to occupy the land and manage the earth for God's kingdom forever and ever *(Psalm 37:9, 11, 29; 115:16; Genesis 1:26; Matthew 5:5; Revelation 5:10; 22:5).*

Jesus is called the Last Adam to remind us that God had not changed His mind concerning us since the time He created the first Adam. His body was given from the earth. God sent Jesus to restore what the first Adam lost. Jesus is called the Last Adam, not the second Adam. There won't be any more Adams, and nothing can change God's original intent for mankind *(1 Corinthians 15:45).*

Believe it or not, our Lord Jesus's purpose is connected to the earth. He has been waiting to come back to earth to rule and reign here. The earth is part of His inheritance, and the life He lives for all eternity is the result of what He did while He was here on the earth. Isn't it ironic that we are waiting to go to heaven, while He is waiting to come back to earth to rule and to reign? *(Psalm 2:7–8; Hebrews 10:12–13).*

We are created as kings. Every time God defines our purpose and identity, He puts kingdom, kings, or royalty first *(Exodus 19:6; 1 Peter 2:9; Revelation 1:6).* He will only relate with mankind in the context of His kingdom. We were created to rule and reign on earth, not in heaven.

> **Then God said, "Let Us make man in Our image, according to Our likeness; let them have dominion over the fish of the sea, over the birds of the air, and over the cattle, over all the earth and over every creeping thing that creeps on the earth."(Genesis 1:26)**

GOD'S ETERNAL PURPOSES

This verse is the purpose statement of mankind. In the Old and New Testaments, God has the same purpose for mankind.

> *And you shall be to Me a kingdom of priests and a holy nation. (Exodus 19:6)*

> *But you are a chosen generation, a royal priesthood, a holy nation, His own special people, that you may proclaim the praises of Him who called you out of darkness into His marvelous light. (1 Peter 2:9)*

> *The heaven, even the heavens, are the Lord's; but the earth He has given to the children of men. (Psalm 115:16)*

> *And have made us kings and priests to our God; and we shall reign on the earth. (Revelation 5:10)*

> *There shall be no night there: They need no lamp nor light of the sun, for the Lord God gives them light. And they shall reign forever and ever. (Revelation 22:5)*

The greatest rebellion of mankind is to go against the purpose of God. When we confess our sins, the first one should be to ask His forgiveness for rebelling against the very purpose for which He created us. When purpose is lost, dysfunction and chaos are inevitable.

God's purpose never changes, but the method, or systems He uses to relate with mankind change from age to age. In the garden, Adam related to God as His Father. Adam was the son of God *(Luke 3:38)*. Each day, when they met together in the garden, it was a family meeting to talk about kingdom business. That's how God wanted to relate with us in His kingdom: as Father and children.

DISCOVERING THE LOST KINGDOM

When Adam fell, he lost this sonship, and God began to use promises, covenants, laws, and grace to deal with mankind. Unfortunately, because of misinformation, people began to focus on the methods and systems instead of the purpose behind them. Below are some of the methods God used to relate with mankind. Even while He employed these, He still related with certain individuals as sons.

- Kingdom
- Father and Son
- Promise (Abraham)
- Covenant (Moses and Israel)
- Law (Old Testament)
- Grace (New Testament)
- Kingdom
- Father and son in the kingdom

Through Jesus, we regained the right to sonship and started to relate with God as Father in His kingdom once again. His purpose concerning mankind remains the same forever and ever. The reason life feels meaningless is because we have neglected God's purpose for our lives and have turned to our own ways. Most of the time, we live for ourselves to gratify the desires of our flesh or to make a livelihood.

This is why people have difficulty understanding God's love. We will find His love in His kingdom. When we neglect his purpose and do our own thing, then He is not responsible for what happens in our lives. Whatever we experience as the consequence of rejecting His purpose, we cannot blame God for it. Outside of His purpose, life on earth is misery.

When God gave the Law to the people of Israel through Moses, the Law was not His purpose. He gave it to man so He would have a basis to relate with them, and for them to relate with Him—so they could potentially fulfill His purpose for their lives. Unfortunately, people made the Law the focus and spent their lives reciting and enforcing it. They made the Law their god. The result was legalism and a religious spirit.

The laws were the terms and conditions of the covenant God made with Israel. As long as they kept the terms and conditions, they prospered. The laws were made for them, not the other way around.

Even today, people make grace their focus. The reason God gave us grace was so we could relate to Him as our Father and He could relate to us as His children, so we could fulfill His purpose for us. However, many people made grace their god and neglected His purpose. As a result, we gained either religious extremism or cheesy grace. Whenever we deviate from God's purpose, life will not go well.

The third eternal purpose of God:

3. EVERY THING GOD CREATED HAS A PURPOSE, PLACE, AND FUNCTION BUILT INTO IT TO FULFILL THAT PURPOSE

Each time God creates something, He defines its purpose and tells it why He is creating it. Then He puts it into a particular place. Everything it needs to fulfill its purpose will be found in the place He puts it.

Additionally, He built within that created thing a function to enable or empower it to fulfill its purpose. For example, God created the fish to swim. When He created fish, He told them what to do. He said, "Swim in the water," and He put the fish in a body of water. That's where fish belong.

DISCOVERING THE LOST KINGDOM

God put the ability to swim in the fish. Fish don't have to go to school to learn to swim. That ability was built into them by God. All a fish is required to do to fulfill its purpose is swim. While it's swimming, all it needs to do to find its food is to keep its eyes and mouth open. God's purpose and plan are that simple. It was never supposed to be strenuous or complicated.

When God created the sun, He defined its purpose by telling it to rule over the day; that's its purpose. Then He put the sun in its proper place. To fulfill its purpose, God built its function on the inside. The chemical reaction necessary to produce heat and light is built within it. It doesn't need to go anywhere to buy something or borrow something. All it needs to do is remain in the place God put it and function.

When God created mankind, He did the same thing. He defined our purpose. Genesis 1:26 is our purpose statement. Then He came down and planted a garden, took the man, and put him in it. That garden was the kingdom of God. That is the place mankind belongs, in God's kingdom.

If a fish leaves the water—the place where God put it and it is supposed to be—what will happen to that fish? It will become prey or die within a few minutes. Remaining in the place God wants us is critical. It is the secret to finding what we need to fulfill our purpose.

When Adam fell, he lost the garden, which was the kingdom of God—the place where God wanted him. Ever since that time, God has been waiting to restore His kingdom to mankind. The verses below show the place where each part of creation belongs:

- Stars of the sky *(Hebrews 11:12)*
- Fish of the sea *(Genesis 1:20, 26)*
- Birds of the air *(Genesis 1:20, 26; Matthew 6:26)*

- Trees of the field *(Leviticus 26:4; Matthew 6:28)*
- Sons of the kingdom *(Luke 3:38; Matthew 8:12, 13:38)*

OUR FOOD IS IN THE KINGDOM OF GOD

When God created Adam, the Bible says He took him and put him in the garden. God knew this man needed God cares about humans more than He cares about other creatures. So why are so many trapped in a survivalist lifestyle? Why do so many humans go hungry and live homeless on food, a place to stay, and other resources to fulfill his assignment. God preplanned and prepared everything. Adam didn't have to worry or go hunting so he could survive.

When Adam arrived in the garden, his food was ready and waiting for him. He didn't have to plant and wait for three weeks or months to harvest and then eat. He needed food the first day he arrived in the garden. His food was waiting and ready to eat. That is why the Word says:

> **Then the Lord God took the man and put him in the garden of Eden to tend and keep it. And the Lord God commanded the man, saying, "Of every tree of the garden you may freely eat." (Genesis 2:15–16)**

God works this way for each human being born on earth. He has an assignment for each individual, and everything they need has been prepared and made ready before they even arrived. Does everyone discover it? No. Does everyone benefit from it? No. We are born into this world with a survivalist mentality. Most people don't discover their kingdom assignment in their lifetime.

Birds have food to eat, fish have plenty to eat in the ocean, and animals in the jungle are full and satisfied. The only group that are hungry, dissatisfied, and die for lack of food are those who are created in the very image and likeness of God. The only creatures that work for their food are humans. Doesn't that sound absurd?

God cares about humans more than He cares about other creatures. So why are so many trapped in a survivalist lifestyle? Why do so many humans go hungry and live homeless on this planet? There's one simple reason: They are not in the place God put them. They are not living in God's kingdom. They are not doing what they were created to do.

Many do this unknowingly because nobody told them why they were created and how to find their kingdom assignment. That is what this book is about. That is why we need to preach the gospel of the kingdom. Mankind needs to rediscover the lost kingdom.

Anytime God called someone to perform an assignment for Him, He provided them with their food.

- Adam in the garden of Eden
- Isaac during famine
- Jacob and his children in Egypt
- Israelites: God provided manna for forty years in the wilderness
- Elijah was fed through a widow and a bird
- Daniel was cared for in captivity
- Disciples: Even after the resurrection, Jesus brought them

In the kingdom prayer, Jesus taught us to pray: Give us this day our daily bread.

GOD'S ETERNAL PURPOSES

It is God's responsibility to provide for those who live in His kingdom. Now that we established the foundation, let's explore more about God's kingdom.

CHAPTER 3

WHAT IS THE KINGDOM?

The Lord has established His throne in heaven, and His kingdom rules over all. (Psalm 103:19)

WHAT IS THE KINGDOM?

As I travel across the world and meet people from different nations, languages, and religions, I have ob- served something very interesting. Every religion is made of the same basic ingredients. Since the fall, whenever man came across something beyond his comprehension, he called it a god. Whether it was water, rock, thunder, wind, the sun, animals, heroes—anything and everything became a god to him. He began to worship the creation rather than worshiping the Creator.

All religions have a story of creation (how the world came to be); they all believe in a god or many gods. They adhere to different types of rituals made of traditions and superstitions to appease that deity. They all believe in good and evil. And finally, they have a belief about what happens after they die or about going to heaven. Thus, various religions were formed.

DISCOVERING THE LOST KINGDOM

Unfortunately, that religious spirit has crept into the church. It has deceived us all about our purpose and our mission on this earth. The purpose behind all religions, including Christianity, is the same—to blind mankind from ever coming to the true knowledge of God and why He created them, and to hide the message of the kingdom from us.

God's kingdom is everlasting and ever expanding. It is the nature of kings to expand their dominion and culture to new territories. For that, He decided to create a new planet called Earth. He wanted someone to take care of and manage that planet for Him, so He created a species called humans, fashioning them in His own image and likeness to fulfill that task. **Mankind's mission was and is to expand and establish the kingdom and the will of God on earth.**

We are created in the image and likeness of God. The word image refers to nature and creativity, and likeness represents similarity, behavior, and capability. **You are created to be like God on the earth.** The more you know about God, the more you are supposed to know about yourself. You were created to function like Him.

Take a journal and write down areas of your life in which you manifest God's image and likeness, areas in which you function like Him. If you don't have much to write down, there is much left to redeem and to be restored.

As God's children, we are supposed to be functioning just like Him (Genesis 1:26; Ephesians 5:1). **We were created to manifest God and His kingdom on earth.** What God is in heaven, we are supposed to be on earth. Knowing God is supposed to help us know more about ourselves, because we are created to be like Him.

If you want to know about yourself—your true identity, purpose, and nature— then study God, because we came from Him. We

WHAT IS THE KINGDOM?

are supposed to be doing on earth what He does in heaven. Our responsibility is to get a glimpse of heaven and make it real on earth.

The Bible says no one has ever seen God *(John 1:18; 1 Timothy 6:16)*. So how do we get to know an invisible God? He chose to manifest Himself in many different ways. First, His attributes and glory are made manifest through the things He created *(Romans 1:20)*.

Each created thing or creature reveals something of His character, glory, nature, or creativity. He chose to manifest His image and likeness through human beings *(Genesis 1:26)*. He revealed His purpose and plan in His Word *(Hebrews 1:1-2)*. Then, at last, He revealed Himself through His only begotten Son, Jesus Christ *(Colossians 1:15)*. So, if someone wants to know God, he or she can know Him through creation, mankind, the Word of God, and by knowing Jesus Christ. When we put all of these revelations together, we will have an idea of who our great God is.

So, what is a kingdom?

A kingdom is a territory or a nation ruled by a king. If there is no territory, and no king, then there is no kingdom. Don't let anyone deceive you. When the Bible mentions the kingdom of God, it is not talking about feelings (emotionalism), going to heaven, church, or a particular type of music.

KINGDOM PERSPECTIVE

Since the kingdom is God's priority, everything He does and says is focused on that one subject. That is why Jesus taught and trained His disciples about the kingdom for more than three years before He ever mentioned anything about the church.

Jesus did not come with a church or revival message. Day and night, His message was all about His Father's kingdom. Then, when

DISCOVERING THE LOST KINGDOM

He realized that the disciples were informed enough about the kingdom, He introduced the concept of the church to them. The church is here to administer the kingdom.

If there is no kingdom, there is no need for a church. The disciples looked at the church from a kingdom perspective; that's why they were so effective in their life in reaching nations. They understood that the purpose of the church was connected to God's kingdom. Today we hear about the church first, and many times don't hear anything about the kingdom at all.

When we hear about the kingdom, we try to look at the kingdom from a church perspective—and we miss the whole thing! If we don't understand the kingdom, we won't understand the purpose of the church. That is exactly what has happened.

Compare this truth with your previous understanding of God's kingdom, or the picture that comes to your mind when you hear the phrase kingdom of God. If that picture does not include a king and a territory He rules, then it is not a kingdom. It is pure religious or utopian ideology.

WHAT IS THE KINGDOM?

A kingdom is made of twelve different components:

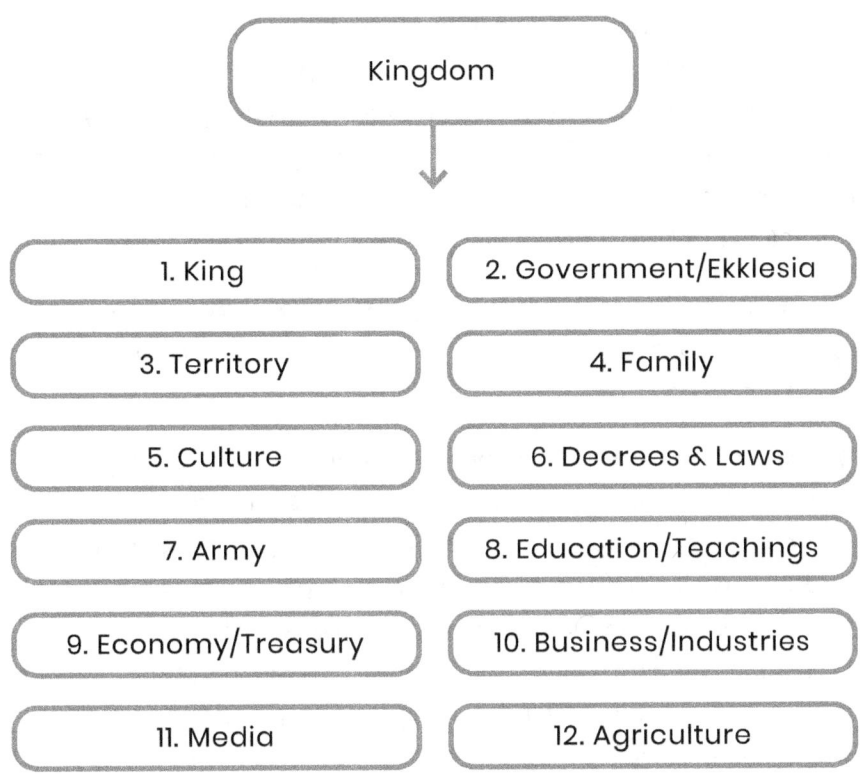

THE DIFFERENCE BETWEEN THE KINGDOM OF GOD AND THE KINGDOM OF HEAVEN

The difference between the kingdom of God and the kingdom of heaven is simple. The first reveals the person to whom the kingdom belongs, and the second shows the place it is located, or where it is from. It is similar to the kingdom of Nebuchadnezzar and the kingdom of Babylon; one shows ownership, and the other shows location.

WHY DID GOD PUT MAN IN A GARDEN?

God needs a specific place to dwell, so He created the heavens. Heaven is His throne *(Psalm 103:19, 115:16)*. He has no plan to share it with anyone else. As we saw earlier, everything God created requires a specific place and has a particular purpose and function. Fish need water; they were created to swim. Birds need air; they were created to fly. And the stars need the sky; they were created to shine. Everything created is connected to a particular place. Where is the place for mankind?

Human beings need the garden of Eden (the kingdom of God), and their purpose is to rule and reign on earth forever *(Genesis 1:26; Revelation 22:5)*.

God knew that the man He was creating would need a place to dwell. God is King; and since we came from God and were made in His image, He created us to be kings *(Revelation 1:6)*. Kings need a kingdom. God came down and planted a garden in the east. The word for "planted" in Hebrew is *nata*, which also means "to establish or fasten."[2] He established His kingdom on earth in the form of a garden. The garden of Eden was the physical manifestation of God's invisible kingdom.

All the components of a kingdom were present in the garden of Eden. There was kingdom economy, education, agriculture, and the nine others. The garden was the prototype of God's kingdom in the visible realm.

When we hear the word garden, we think of plants and trees with flowers and fruit. The garden of Eden was much more than a mere

---

[2] James Strong, "5193. Nata," Strong's Hebrew: 5193. נָטַע (nata) -- to plant, (Biblehub), https://biblehub.com/hebrew/5193.htm.

WHAT IS THE KINGDOM?

garden that we see in our day and time. Though it might have had plants and trees, it was a meeting place for God and man and the meeting point between heaven and earth. It was an extension of the kingdom of heaven to earth. It was the gate of heaven. It was an atmosphere and environment created by God for both Him and man to function together in an intimate relationship and partnership. It was God's kingdom manifested in visible form.

The word used for "garden" in Hebrew is gan, which means "an enclosure or a protected environment."[3] It was a protected or secured environment, and it was Adam's responsibility to protect it from any intruders. The garden of Eden was the headquarters, or the command center, of the kingdom of heaven for the whole earth. God's will and plan for man was to make the entire earth just like Eden. Man's job was to duplicate and expand what God had done there. Just like we learned to think of heaven as a kingdom, when we refer to the garden of Eden, learn to think of it as a kingdom.

God's will was done in Eden as it was in heaven. If you could mess Eden up, you could mess up the entire plan of God for the earth. If we removed ourselves from Eden or if we lost it, we would miss the plan for the entire planet.

That's what happened with the fall of mankind. The enemy lured us with the fruit and stole the garden from us. We lost the garden, and with that, we lost the kingdom of God. We lost the blueprint and rulership of the earth, and temporarily messed up the plan of God for the earth and humans.

God created man to live in His kingdom, and ever since man lost the garden or the kingdom of God, we have been on a search for it

---

[3] James Strong, "1588. Gan." Strong's Hebrew: 1588. גן (Gan) -- an Enclosure, Garden, (Biblehub), www.biblehub.com/hebrew/1588.htm.

throughout the centuries. You will read more about this in the next chapter. **It is impossible for mankind to live without a kingdom because we are created as kings (1 Peter 2:9; Revelation 1:6; 5:10).**

There are three kingdoms operating on the earth right now. Every human being depends on one of them: the kingdom of God, the kingdom of darkness, or the kingdoms of men *(Daniel 4:17, 25)*.

Genesis 1:26 is the purpose statement for man that was given by our Creator.

> *Then God said, "Let Us make man in Our image, according to Our likeness; let them have dominion over the fish of the sea, over the birds of the air, and over the cattle, over all the earth and over every creeping thing that creeps on the earth."*

Man was created to subdue and rule the earth and everything in it. Many think that Genesis 1 and 2 are creation stories. They are not stories; they are God's original blueprint, His design for the earth and mankind. If we do not understand Genesis 1 and 2, we will not understand our purpose on earth—or the rest of the Bible.

There are many who believe that Genesis 1:26-28 is not applicable to mankind today because they think God changed His mind. They say this because they don't understand the true meaning of dominion. To the western mind, dominion means "to take over, invade, oppress, enslave by force." That is domination, not dominion. Domination is demonic; dominion is of the kingdom.

WHAT IS DOMINION?

The entire Bible is about a King, His kingdom, and His royal family. He decided to extend that kingdom to a planet called Earth. To manage

WHAT IS THE KINGDOM?

that kingdom, He created a unique species in His image and likeness called human beings. That is our purpose: to represent God and manage His kingdom on earth.

The King's first mandate to man was to have dominion over the earth and everything He created in it *(Genesis 1:26)*. According to the law of first mention, when God speaks about something for the first time, He reveals His heart and purpose concerning that thing.

A mandate is an authorization to act, a charge to get things done, a commission to carry out an injunction, a precept to which to adhere, a guideline to follow without deviation, and an important order that must be obeyed. God gave the mandate to Adam and Eve to have dominion over the earth and subdue and rule everything God created. But Adam failed in his assignment.

Man was deceived by the enemy and lost his dominion over the earth. Still, God did not change His purpose concerning man or His kingdom. He chose individuals and then a nation—the nation of Israel—to represent Him and His kingdom on earth. Eventually, they also rebelled and failed in their assignment. So Jesus said,

> **Therefore I say to you, the kingdom of God will be taken from you (Israel), and given to a nation (the church) bearing the fruits of it. (Matthew 21:43)**

In the verse above, Jesus says the kingdom of God will be taken from the people of Israel and given to a nation. The church is a holy nation in itself, a nation within the nation you are living in *(1 Peter 2:9)*. The church is supposed to function like a nation, like the nation of Israel used to function.

God sent His Son to die for our sins and to reinstate His kingdom purpose. He instituted the church, comprised of both Jews and gentiles, to represent Him and His kingdom. This is not a new revelation I just discovered or made up. The revelation of God's kingdom is as old as the heavens and the earth.

Throughout the centuries, the church has been asking God for particular benefits and specializing in a few aspects of the kingdom instead of crying out for His kingdom to come. As a result, He sent the Salvation Movement, Healing Movement, Holiness Movement, Word of Faith Movement, and others. These are all different aspects of His kingdom, but not the whole kingdom. The time has come for us to receive the whole kingdom and administer it so God's will is done on the earth as it is in heaven. It is time for a Kingdom Movement!

Dominion is delegated authority or the right to rule.

Dominion is a kingdom word. Kings have kingdoms, and kingdoms have dominion. Dominion refers to the authority or the right to rule. It is the birthright of each and every human being, given by our Creator, not just some special race or family. If you are part of God's kingdom, you belong to a royal family.

Dominion comes as part of your birthright. You were born with the right to rule this planet and all the creatures God created. It has been given to us by our God and Creator. You don't need to be a Christian, speak in tongues, get baptized, or belong to any church to have dominion. You don't even have to believe in God. Sometimes the church will try to brainwash you out of your birthright in the kingdom. Many so-called ministers have been successful in creating orphans who feel as though it is illegal to be on this planet and do anything here.

This inheritance came as part of your birth. Most believers don't believe this because they have been brainwashed by the religious system in which they were brought up in. Do not give away your birthright.

WHAT IS THE KINGDOM?

Don't sell or surrender it. If you do, you won't have the resources to fulfill your assignment. The resources you need to fulfill your assignment are part of your birthright in the kingdom.

They will come to you only if you exercise the mandate of dominion. If you give it away or sell it, you will be like a vagabond.

Esau sold his birthright for a cup of stew. He didn't value it but sold it for temporary gratification. Later he cried out for a blessing, but there was none left. He and his descendants were cut off from the face of the earth. God hates those who sell or give away their birthright because birthright comes from Him. He gave it to you. You are not supposed to give away something that you did not earn.

You don't need to be born again to go to the moon. You don't need to be speaking in tongues to run a global business. You don't need to be a member of a church or even be saved to invent something. You don't need to sing songs to manufacture a product. Just being human qualifies you to do all that. However, you do need to learn and maximize your potential by exercising the first mandate God gave us— dominion.

One thing about the earth is this: You need to harness its potential to extract its resources. It won't just give you its gold as you walk by. Trees won't produce furniture for you. Metals won't manufacture cars for you. Stones won't come together and build you a house. Diamonds won't make you a nice piece of jewelry, and gold won't make a chain for you on its own.

You have to exert energy, use your creativity, and maximize your productivity and potential to make what you want. You have to put a demand on resources. You have to put a demand on your potential and the potential of the earth. That's how you need to exercise your birthright of dominion.

DISCOVERING THE LOST KINGDOM

This is the reason most people remain poor all their life. They are all waiting for a miracle; they are all waiting to receive something for free. They want somebody to give things to them: their food, house, cars, and so on. They have been ignorant of their birthright given by God.

Our number one problem is our church mindset. The concept we have of church is skewed. If you are part of the current church system, I can guarantee that you have some strongholds. Nothing kills creativity and steals destinies more than religion.

If you look at any aspect of life with a church mindset, you won't have the correct perspective. Because the church concept is so messed up, everything we look at through that religious lens will be tainted as well.

Every human being has the equal authority and right to rule this planet, but we won't all rule the same way. Only one person can be the president of a country at any given time, but each one of us is created to rule over at least one area of life.

God specified what He was expecting us to do in Genesis 1:26. First, He told us to take dominion over the fish of the sea. We were created to rule over anything related to the ocean: the water, the sea, and the creatures in it. Any time we see rebellion, God said to subdue it and rule over it.

Next, God spoke of the birds of the air. We are to reign over the bird kingdom or the airwaves. This includes anything related to it: aviation, airwaves, and the wind; anything that works with the wind is our domain.

Then God referenced all the cattle. We are not supposed to worship the cattle; every animal is under our domain. Then He mentioned

WHAT IS THE KINGDOM?

the earth. We were created to rule anything related to the earth: economy, politics, government, natural resources, minerals, oil, trees, precious stones, metals, and anything else.

God spoke of every creeping thing that creeps on the earth. Anything that moves on this planet is under our jurisdiction, and we have the authority and the right to rule over it. We have been given the right to rule (or maximize) anything that is of value that our heavenly Father has deposited here for His kingdom advancement.

Remember, God did not include people in the list of creatures mentioned in Genesis 1:26 that was commanded by Him to Adam.

We are not supposed to rule over people; we were created to be governed by Him.

Jesus shared two parables that should frighten all the rapture-waiting believers around the globe. They are the parable of the talents and the parable of the vineyard. God has given us resources, wealth, and the whole earth for a lease. Every lease has an expiration date. When He comes back, He wants to see the earth better than it was when He gave it to us. Whatever God gives us, He wants it back and multiplied. If it has not become better, then we will be sorry when He comes *(Matthew 21:33–41, 25:14–29)*.

God won't put a demand on something or someone in which He has not first made a deposit. If He has required something from you, He is sure you can produce it.

That's why Revelation 11:18 says that when He comes, He will destroy those who destroyed the earth. God created and put us here to take care of this planet. We were created for the planet, not the other way around. If this whole planet is being kept for fire, why would God care about it? Why would He destroy those who destroy the earth?

That's something to think about. The earth is His kingdom property. If we don't take care of it, He will deal with us without any mercy.

The word *dominion* is very complex. I wrote about it with its twelve definitions, and the process of having dominion, in more detail in my book Discovering Purpose, Calling, and Gifts.

THE KINGDOM IS OUR BIRTHRIGHT

The kingdom of God is our birthright. Everyone has the right to live in God's kingdom, but man has a choice. We can choose to live in God's kingdom, build our own kingdom, or build the kingdom of darkness. No matter what, we are kingdom builders.

Adam didn't have to do anything to qualify for the garden of Eden. Just being born as God's son was enough qualification to be in the kingdom. He didn't perform any religious rituals. The kingdom was prepared for him when he arrived.

It is the same today. It is our Father's good pleasure to give us the kingdom *(Luke 12:32)*. We don't need to do any Pentecostal gymnastics to qualify for His kingdom. However, we do have to unlearn everything we learned from religion, culture, education, and our previous experiences to enter His kingdom. That is why Jesus said we have to repent to receive the kingdom. To "repent" means to change the way we think.

Most people spend more than twelve years in school to learn the ways of this world. If you went to college, even more years were added to that. When we come into the kingdom, we have to unlearn everything we learned before that time so we can enter it. Everything the church has taught us that was not of the kingdom has to be unlearned as well, so it takes us a while.

WHAT IS THE KINGDOM?

That's why most people won't receive the kingdom, and it also explains why it seems confusing to them in the beginning. They are programmed in the ways of this world and religion, so it's difficult for them to comprehend the ways of God. The disciples had to unlearn everything about the old covenant and give up their fishing business to be part of Jesus's kingdom. The Pharisees were not willing to give up what they knew and what they had been practicing for centuries. They missed both the kingdom and God's plan for them.

The garden of Eden was the physical manifestation of the kingdom of God on earth. When Adam fell, he lost it. The new covenant is all about the restoration of God's kingdom, mankind, and the whole earth.

CHAPTER 4
THE CREATION AND FALL OF MAN-KIND

The crown has fallen from our head. Woe to us, for we have sinned! (Lamentation 5:16)

We have learned that God created man to have dominion or rule over the earth. That is our eternal purpose in relation to His kingdom. To accomplish that goal, God gave Adam all he needed. That is a kingdom principle. Whatever you need to fulfill your assignment comes with the assignment. You don't need to try to make it happen on your own. Below are the things God gave Adam when He created him.

1. IMAGE AND LIKENESS OF GOD (GENESIS 1:26)

As mentioned earlier, we are like God on the earth. The enemy is trying everything he can to corrupt the image and likeness of God in humans. He wants to corrupt the seed of man so that he can thwart the purpose of God. He tried that once in Genesis when the angels began to intermingle with the daughters of men and produced superhuman beings. God had to destroy that entire race with a flood.

Now through genetic manipulation and artificial intelligence, scientists are producing beings that are not fully human. They are injecting male hormones into women and female hormones into men through vaccines and foods people eat. As a result, there are people out there who are neither fully male nor female.

2. GOD'S SPIRIT OR THE BREATH OF LIFE (GENESIS 2:7; JOB 33:4)

God gave us His Spirit to dwell in us so we could connect with Him. God is Spirit, and those connected with Him and worshiping Him must do so in spirit. Our body is the conduit for Him to accomplish His purpose on the earth through His Spirit.

3. SONSHIP-RELATIONSHIP WITH GOD (LUKE 3:38)

Sonship is our identity and birthright in the kingdom. Adam was born a son of God. He did not have to do anything specific or perform any rituals to become a son of God or before meeting with Him. It is the same in the New Testament. God gave us each the right to become His child *(John 1:12)*. This is not based on church affiliation or how many times you praise the Lord each day.

4. GLORY OF GOD (ROMANS 3:23)

One thing we lost when Adam fell was the glory of God. We were created to live in His glory; it was our covering. Adam and Eve did not feel any shame, fear, or insecurity as long as they lived in His glory. It is a place where we lack nothing in our lives. God restored His glory to us through Jesus Christ.

5. DOMINION OVER THE ENTIRE EARTH (GENESIS 1:26)

Dominion is our purpose. It is the first mandate God gave to mankind. If we do not obey the first mandate, then nothing else will work well for us. Everything will be out of order and balance, which is what we see around us.

6. WEALTH AND RESOURCES (GENESIS 2:10-14)

Everything Adam needed to fulfill His purpose was provided for Him by God. All wealth and every resource was placed in the earth by God to be used to build His kingdom. Unfortunately, the enemy is the one using most of it to build his kingdom. This must change.

7. THE GARDEN (GENESIS 2:8,15)

The garden was the place to dwell for Adam and Eve. God didn't build a skyscraper but planted a garden for the first family.

8. THE KINGDOM OF GOD (GENESIS 2:8,15)

As we learned earlier, the garden was the kingdom of God. God's will was done in Eden as it is in heaven.

9. FOOD (GENESIS 1:29; 2:16)

When you commit yourself to the assignment God created to you do, He is faithful to provide what you need, just like He did for Adam and others in the Bible.

10. FAMILY (GENESIS 2:21-22)

We were created for relationships. Marriage is God's idea; it is a kingdom concept designed to fulfill a kingdom assignment.

Outside of His kingdom, marriage won't work. We will learn more about this later.

WHAT WE LOST

Many people are worried and concerned about the end times because they don't know the beginning well. The Bible ends where it began. If you want to know the end, look at the beginning. What I mean is this, Genesis 1 and 2 reveal God's original plan for man and the earth. It got messed up, and ever since that time, He has been restoring us to His original intent. Revelation 21 and 22 take us back to the beginning once again. If we don't understand the beginning, we will not understand the present or the end.

We wasted many generations waiting for the end of the world or the rapture. We have been robbed and cheated by the devil through the religious spirit. As a result, we lost nations, our inheritance, family, and governments—almost everything! It is time to restart and go back to the very beginning. Let's shake off our religious masks and put on Christ and see through his eyes the world He created.

Mankind was deceived by our enemy, Satan. Through deception, humans disobeyed God, and sin and death entered them and planet Earth. Sin is the operating system of the kingdom of darkness. It is a Satanic Information Network (SIN). All sin originates as a thought or imagination. Every thought or imagination that is in contradiction to God's Word comes from SIN. When sin entered humans, they lost the ability to think right and to see themselves as God sees them. Instead, they inherited a wrong view of themselves, God, and the earth— and were swayed from their purpose.

Man was created to live wholly dependent on God and His kingdom. The first temptation of Satan was to allure man to think and

THE CREATION AND FALL OF MAN-KIND

operate independently of God, which gave birth to humanism and individualism. Humanism is the tendency of mankind to trust in themselves and put themselves in the place of God.

Mankind looked for knowledge and enlightenment apart from God, after tasting the fruit of the tree of the knowledge of good and evil. Know that there was some good in that tree in the beginning, but that good eventually turned into evil because God was not in it. There is some good in almost everything, but we need to look at the end and where it will ultimately lead us. If something does not lead us to life, it is not worth pursuing. Man's hunger for knowledge apart from God also gave birth to Gnosticism *(Genesis 3:6)*.

After the fall, man and woman lost the glory of God and realized they were naked. They sewed fig leaves and covered their nakedness. They began to depend on their works to be accepted by God or to please Him. This gave birth to religion because sin distorts our view of God and His character.

ISRAEL AND THE EKKLESIA

After the fall of mankind, to accomplish His will on earth God chose a man named Abraham. Through his descendants, Jacob and his twelve sons, God established a nation called Israel. Israel became the physical manifestation on earth of God's invisible kingdom. Anyone who saw Israel knew they were special and different from all other nations. They were blessed above all others.

God's plan was to bless the earth and all the nations through the Israelites. He wanted them to be the light to the gentiles and cover the earth with His glory, but they didn't want to share the blessing. They kept it for themselves and eventually rejected the God who had blessed them *(Genesis 12:3, 22:18; Isaiah 42:6)*.

DISCOVERING THE LOST KINGDOM

Israel was God's garden (or kingdom) manifested. It was the gate of heaven, and God accomplished His will and plan on earth through them. But their glory did not last long either. Because they disobeyed God, they were taken captive by other nations and lost the blessings and the land God gave them.

God decided to create another *nation* to fulfill His counsel and purpose throughout the earth. He chose another twelve Jewish men to establish this new nation. The Jewish people rejected His plan again, but their rejection became a blessing to the gentiles *(Romans 11:11–32)*. God took the blessing He planned to share through them to the rest of the world, and gave it to the gentiles to do it. He extended His invitation and blessings to everyone from every nation to be part of this new nation.

This nation has the same purpose Israel had, which is to accomplish His will on earth and to be the light of this world and salt of the earth. God did not choose Abraham or Israel to populate heaven, nor did He create the church for that purpose. Our purpose is to fill the earth with the knowledge of His glory. I will explain more about this later in the book.

Jesus chose twelve men to establish this new nation *(Matthew 21:43; 1 Peter 2:9)*. In the Bible, the number twelve signifies government. Jesus trained these twelve men and sent them out to preach the good news of the kingdom to the four corners of the earth. Everyone who received and believed the good news and the Lord Jesus Christ was added to them, forming this new nation.

That nation is called the church, or *ekklesia*. He decided to operate through the church to establish His will and kingdom on earth. Just like Adam and Israel, the church has not done a good job in fulfilling

THE CREATION AND FALL OF MAN-KIND

its assignment. It is far from establishing His will and kingdom on earth. Instead, most church members are waiting to disappear from the earth.

The church is supposed to be the visible manifestation of the invisible kingdom. Those who see the church should understand and know how the kingdom of God operates. That was the case in Eden and the nation of Israel, and the early church.

Whatever the garden of Eden was, Israel became just that. Now, whatever Israel was, the church became just that or, at least, it is supposed to become that. The church is the gate of heaven, a meeting place for man and God. Whatever God wants to accomplish on the earth, He wants to do it through the church.

Whenever something tragic happens, Christians usually say, "God is in control, don't worry, be happy." They say this out of their ignorance and religious deception. God is not in the controlling business. If God was in control, Adam would still be in the garden. He is in the business of giving people a choice.

Everything we experience now on earth is the total sum of all the decisions and choices mankind made, beginning with Adam. Everything we experience personally is a result of all of the choices we made in our lives. We can't blame God for them.

When Adam decided to sin, God did not step in to stop him. When he committed sin and fell, he lost seven things— and it affected all of creation. Below are the seven things we lost and the verses which show how God restored what we lost through Jesus Christ.

WHAT ADAM LOST WHEN HE FELL

1. BIRTHRIGHT

The enemy knew that what qualified Adam to own what he owned and do what he was doing was his birthright. Everything God gave to him came because of his birthright. The enemy knew that if he could steal that from him, he could, in turn, have what Adam had and do what Adam was created to do. That is exactly what happened through deception. The enemy stole Adam's birthright; and with that, Adam lost everything God gave to him. He became an orphan and illegal in the garden.

That is why believers feel like they don't belong on the earth. Once you lose your birthright, you lose your citizenship, and you become illegal in a country. The enemy used our birthright and began to do on earth what God told Adam to do. Since then, the seed of the wicked has been ruling the earth while the righteous are waiting to escape.

This is why the first thing God restores to us when we believe in Jesus is our birthright. Whoever believes in and receives Jesus, God gives them the right to become a child of God *(John 1:12)*. But many misunderstand it as a ticket to get into heaven.

2. SONSHIP

When Adam met with God in the garden each day, he met with Him on the basis of a son meeting his Father. There was no singing, music, or any kind of ritual necessary to meet his heavenly Father. Adam was the son of God *(Luke 3:38)*. When he sinned, he could not face God anymore as His son. Fear and shame came into his heart and he felt rejected by God. He couldn't see God as his Father. He felt like an orphan. The truth was that God did not change a bit; it

THE CREATION AND FALL OF MAN-KIND

was Adam's perception of God that changed. That's what sin does to our hearts and our perception of God.

3. RIGHT TO RULE THE EARTH

As a result of mankind's fall, the devil stole our birthright and received the right to rule the earth. He empowered his children to rule, even though ruling was our birthright. Even now, the ungodly are ruling this planet, while the righteous are waiting for a fire evacuation. God never intended for the wicked to hold any position of authority on this planet.

4. GOD'S SPIRIT

Man was filled with the Spirit of God and was led by Him. Mankind lost Him. That's why we need to be refilled with His Spirit.

5. PROVISION AND DWELLING PLACE

Food and accommodation were part of the kingdom assignment God gave to Adam. When he fell, he lost them.

His life was in his own hands, and he had to work hard to earn what he was going to eat and to find where he was going to dwell.

6. GLORY OF GOD

Man was created to live in God's glory or the glory realm. He didn't feel any shame or inadequacy as long as he lived in God's glory. Sin caused man to fall short of God's glory, but Jesus gave it back to those who chose Him *(Romans 3:23)*.

7. KINGDOM OF GOD

The garden was the visible manifestation of God's kingdom on earth. When Adam lost the garden, he lost the kingdom with it.

8. THE TREE OF LIFE

Man was created to live forever by eating from the tree of life. After the fall God chased Adam and Eve away from the garden so that they wouldn't reach out and eat from the tree of life and live in the fallen state forever.

RELATIONSHIPS AFFECTED BY THE FALL

1. RELATIONSHIP BETWEEN MAN AND GOD

After the fall, Adam and Eve couldn't face God or stand before Him. They hid themselves among the bushes. They lost their sonship. Through Christ, we have been reconciled and have made peace with God *(Romans 5:1; 2 Corinthians 5:18)*.

2. RELATIONSHIP BETWEEN HEAVEN AND EARTH

Heaven and earth functioned as one before the fall. Man could easily move from one realm to the next with ease. The natural and the spiritual were in perfect unity and felt as one to Adam.

Adam and Eve could see into the heavens and tap into what they needed. After the fall, that relationship was also broken. There was a separation between heaven and earth, and the natural and the spiritual. Man lost the ability to tap into the spiritual. He became a mere natural being.

Through the death of Jesus on the cross, God reconciled things in heaven and things on earth *(Ephesians 1:10; Colossians 1:20)*. Once again, man had access to the things of the Spirit. However, too many tap into the demonic world instead.

THE CREATION AND FALL OF MAN-KIND

3. RELATIONSHIP BETWEEN MAN AND NATURE

Nature is supposed to function in partnership with mankind to accomplish God's will on earth. Nature also is supposed to represent His kingdom. After the fall, nature began to rebel and rule over us instead. Through Christ, we received the dominion mandate once again. That is why Psalm 8:6 says He made us to rule over the works of His hands.

4. RELATIONSHIP WITHIN MANKIND

We are spirit beings living in a body and we have a soul. We were led by our spirit before the fall. Once Adam fell, our mind and body took over and began to tell us what to do and how to live. Our body was given to house our spirit and God's Spirit, not to tell us what to do. Once we are saved, we are supposed to be led by our spirit. However, it takes time to tame our mind and body and bring them under subjection to our spirit and God's Spirit.

5. RELATIONSHIP WITH OTHERS

There was only one race before the fall—the human race. As people began to multiply based on which part of the earth they dwelt, different colors and sizes of people began to emerge. They became divided into different ethnic and language groups.

Once we are saved, we regain the citizenship of our country of origin. We become part of the same family and citizens of the same kingdom.

6. RELATIONSHIP WITH THE DEMONIC WORLD

Before the fall, the demonic world had no right to rule on the earth. Demons had access to the earth realm, but they had no right to afflict, torment, or possess humans. The fall of Adam, and sin, gave them the right to possess humans and operate through them to manifest their evil nature. They also received the right to establish their kingdom on earth.

But through salvation, we regain our birthright and authority over demons to cancel any rights or authority they gained. After the resurrection, Jesus received all authority on earth and in heaven. Through Him, we have power and authority over the entire demonic world *(Luke 10:19)*.

7. THE BONDAGE OF CORRUPTION (ROMANS 8:19-21)

The fall not only affected mankind, but all of creation. The whole creation came under the bondage of death and corruption.

GOD HAS NOT GIVEN UP

Because of the fall, the righteous lost the rulership and dominion over the earth. Satan took hold of the opportunity and began to establish his kingdom and will on earth through his children. The earth is the Lord's property, and He gave it to His children *(Psalm 115:16)*, but because of deception and the fall, the righteous lost dominion over the earth.

God never intended that the wicked would be in any position of authority. That is why the Bible says that when the righteous are in authority the city rejoices, but when the wicked rule, people groan (Proverbs 29:2).

Thankfully, God did not give up on us. He was committed to saving mankind and restoring us to His original intent. To accomplish that, He introduced the plan of salvation through His Son Jesus Christ. Salvation is not just about making it to heaven after we die. In the next chapter, we are going to see the process of salvation God instituted to restore everything we lost.

CHAPTER 5

THE PROCESS OF SALVATION

Work out your own salvation with fear and trembling.
(Philippians 2:12)

WHAT IS SALVATION?

Salvation is realigning us with God's original intent for the earth and mankind, and restoring our relationship with Him as our Father and King, thereby regaining everything we lost because of the fall of Adam.

When you are saved, if nothing was restored that Adam lost, then you didn't understand the purpose of salvation or what salvation is all about. To restore everything we lost through the fall of Adam, God instituted a plan to save us. Salvation is not about barely making it to heaven when you die; it's about how much you would like to redeem what the enemy stole from you. If you don't know what you lost, then how will you know what to receive back? We saw what we lost because of the fall of Adam in the previous chapter.

DISCOVERING THE LOST KINGDOM

One thing must be understood: Salvation is generational. What do I mean by that? It will take more than one generation to take back everything we lost when Adam fell. It took hundreds of generations for us to get to where we are today. To reverse and restore everything will take more time. Each generation needs to pass the baton, so restoration can be taken to the next level.

God promised Abraham that He would make him a great nation. Abraham did not become a nation in his lifetime. It took five generations for his descendants to become a nation in Egypt, and many more until they were delivered and reached the Promised Land to establish a political nation. Each generation had a part to fulfill.

When David died, he passed the baton to his son Solomon, who took the kingdom of Israel to a whole new level. But Solomon didn't set a good example. After him, the downfall started. Since the fall of Adam, our intellectual capacity, creativity, and longevity have deteriorated from generation to generation.

When Christ died on the cross, He reconciled us back to God and healed the relationships between things in heaven and things on earth. From that time until now, life was supposed to be getting better in every way. In some ways it did get better, but we neglected many areas. Heaven was supposed to be manifested more and more on the earth, but that changed over time. By the mid-1800s, the church embraced the idea that we are waiting for the rapture to go to heaven.

The rapture syndrome has greatly damaged the body of Christ and made us ineffective. It created an escapist mentality; in that mindset, we neglected our nations and communities and began to sit and watch what the devil and his children were doing, which we talk about when we meet in a building that we call a church. That's not the reason Jesus started His church.

Unfortunately, unbelievers began to tap into the benefits that were made available to us—without even knowing it—and began to advance in every arena of life. They took them and ran with them while believers are still waiting for another miracle. Lord, have mercy!

Once our spirit is saved, we need to start working out the salvation of our soul, then our body, and then the community around us *(Philippians 2:12)*. Salvation is for the whole world, not just human souls. All of creation, and every creature, was affected by the fall of Adam. They all need to experience salvation. We've limited salvation to escaping hell.

After we are saved, our family needs to be saved, then our government needs to be saved, then our economy, education system, agriculture, every nation, and finally, the whole creation. That's what Jesus told us to do by discipling nations *(Matthew 28:19)* and preaching the gospel to every creature *(Mark 16:15)*.

Now let's look at the process the Bible teaches that each individual must go through to receive everything we lost.

THE PROCESS OF SALVATION

Many believers feel empty and lost inside, even while being members of a church. They have no idea why they are here. They've been tormented by the enemy day and night and are struggling to survive. There are four reasons this happens.

First, they have not gone through the process of salvation. Second, they have not yet discovered the kingdom. Third, they are not walking in their calling. And the fourth reason is because they have not identified their gifts. Instead, they are trying to copy someone else. Many are waiting for Jesus to come and save them again.

DISCOVERING THE LOST KINGDOM

I want to take a deeper look at the first reason: they have not gone through the process of salvation. What do I mean by that? Salvation does not end when you are *born again.* That's only the first step. The next step is deliverance *(Colossians 1:13).*

Many have limited salvation to a ticket to heaven. It's become a get-out- of-jail-free card and nothing more. But salvation is much bigger than just reaching heaven. The plan of salvation will not be completed until we regain *everything* that was lost through the fall of Adam. To help us accomplish that, God implemented a six-step process. When we complete that process, we can say we are completely saved.

1. BORN A GAIN

As a result, we regain our citizenship and we will see the country of our origin *(John 3:3; 1 Peter 1:23).* By natural birth, we became citizens of a country. By spiritual birth, we regain our kingdom citizenship. Your citizenship comes with certain rights. As a citizen, you have rights and privileges that a visitor does not have. You can vote, you can buy property, you can work, you can start businesses, you can be part of the government, and so on.

Why does God want you to be born again? This is a spiritual phenomenon as well as a kingdom phenomenon. The main reason God wants you to be born again is that He wants you to be a citizen of a new country. When you were born again, you became a citizen of the kingdom of heaven. That is why Paul says our real citizenship is not on earth but in heaven *(Philippians 3:20).* This is the first step in the process.

2. REPENTANCE

The action or the process of returning to our original way of thinking by renewing our mind with the Word of God *(Romans 12:2).* The more

THE PROCESS OF SALVATION

we renew our mind with the Word, the more life in the kingdom becomes real to us. If our way of thinking has not changed, then we have only confessed our sins. Many people confuse repentance with confession.

Since we are born into a new kingdom, it is our responsibility to learn to think according to the customs and culture of this new kingdom. To *repent* means to go back to how Adam used to think before the fall. To *renew* means to have something go back to its original state, like when it was new.

3. DELIVERANCE

We must deactivate, disconnect, and destroy every influence of the devil and his kingdom from our life—beginning with our conception, DNA, birth, and birthright (*Romans 7:6; Colossians 1:13; 1 Thessalonians 1:10*).

Every individual needs to experience deliverance. If you don't think you need to be delivered from anything, it's because of pride—so you need to be delivered from pride first! What we think is normal in our life and culture is not normal in the kingdom of God. When the deliverance process is over, our whole being will be fully in the kingdom of God.

There are some major areas from which each one of us needs to be delivered. I am listing fifteen of them here. When we are free in these areas, other strongholds will become easy to deal with. These are root issues that give the enemy a legal right to mess up our lives.

> **The opinion of others:** I'm not sure how many people have forfeited what God has for them because they listened to other people's opinions. People will have an opinion about everything. We should not live our life based on the opinions

of others. In some cultures, when God tells a person to do something, the first thing they think about is what a certain person will think if they obey God. They live to please people rather than God.

Religious spirit: Everyone needs to be free from the religious spirit, regardless of the church background they grew up in. Those who are influenced by this spirit won't know their purpose or the purpose of the earth. They are more committed to and focused on keeping their religious practices. They are not worshiping God; they are worshiping the religious rituals themselves, which in turn become their god.

How do you know if a person is serving a religious spirit or the true living God? There is a very simple test to know the difference. If that person blindly keeps doing the same religious rituals and traditions over and over again for decades, they are not serving the living God

The spirit of this world: The spirit of this world is the opposite of the religious spirit. The religious spirit thrives in rituals and outward appearances, while the spirit of this world thrives on having fun and a false sense of freedom or independence. Those who are influenced by this spirit are always looking for something fun to do. People become more passionate about a sports team than the God who gave them life. They will do crazy things or whatever their flesh wants to do, and they will proclaim that they are free and wild.

Spirit of mammon: According to Jesus, there are only two masters: God and mammon. We either serve God with our lives or we spend our lives trying to make money. Jesus said we can't serve two masters; we love one and hate the other.

THE PROCESS OF SALVATION

What do we spend the majority of our time on earth doing? Do we serve God, or try to make money to survive?

If the sole purpose of our existence is to make a little more money to survive, then we need to be free from the spirit of mammon.

Spirit of lust: Lust is the root of all sin. All sin originates with fleshly lust. There is a spirit called lust. When we feel unnatural desire or inordinate love toward someone or something, know that this spirit is at work.

Spirit of individualism: We live in an individualistic culture where people think they are free to do whatever they want to do. That is not kingdom living. Isaac was not born to do whatever he wanted to do. He was born into a promise that God gave to his father, Abraham. Our life is supposed to be a continuation of the last generation. They are supposed to pass the baton to us, and we are supposed to continue the journey. Later on, when Jacob was born, he was the next in line to carry out the task of fulfilling God's promises, not try to become a soccer player instead.

This is what happens in many modern families. The parents have no clue what their kingdom assignment is, so they raise their children to do whatever they want. There is no vision for the family as a whole. They are more influenced by the world and its heroes than by the kingdom of God.

Individualism crept into the church and destroyed the generational blessings of many. They are out there trying to make it happen or trying to prove something, but at the end of their lives, they feel broken and unfulfilled.

Spirit of pleasure: People have become lovers of pleasure rather than lovers of God.

Fears and insecurities: I have not met anyone yet who isn't afraid of something. But don't let those fears stop you or steal your kingdom destiny. God knows our fears, which is why He tells us again and again not to fear. Fear is a spirit.

Spirit of poverty: Many people think their biggest problem is a lack of money. They believe that if they had a lot of money, then they could do what God has called them to do. They feel this way because they are affected by the spirit of poverty. There's not even one example in the Bible of someone who didn't do what they were called to do because they didn't have enough money. What we need to do is get free from this spirit.

Healing from emotional wounds and traumas: All of us were brought up in some kind of dysfunction. We may have father or mother wounds, sibling wounds, or wounds that were caused by someone in authority. Those abuses, wounds, and traumas left scars in our soul, and we tend to look at life and others through the twisted perspective or glasses formed by those scars.

People go through unimaginable and unexplainable things while growing up. We need to deal with each of those issues and find healing if we are going to regain our right vision and our true identity.

These are major strongholds that give demons an entrance or even residence in a person's life. There are other strongholds like anger, hatred, bitterness, unforgiveness, and curses that allow an open door to the enemy. That's why I said above that deliverance has to start with our bloodline and DNA. Keep in mind that deliverance is an ongoing process until our last day on the earth.

THE PROCESS OF SALVATION

Once we start going through deliverance in the areas of our lives mentioned above, we can move on to the next process of salvation. We can't go into the next process until we have dealt with repentance and deliverance. If we do, we will face backlash from the enemy. Do not go into the battle while the enemy still has legal rights over your life. That is not wise.

4. REDEMPTION

This refers to receiving or buying back everything we lost or was stolen from us *(1 Corinthians 1:30; Galatians 3:13; Hebrews 9:12; 1 Peter 1:18)*. After deliverance, we need to experience redemption. Redemption is buying back what we lost. Jesus paid the price through His blood to buy back everything the enemy stole from us. Now it is up to us how much we want to receive back.

5. RESTORATION

This is returning something or someone to its original owner, position, purpose, and function *(Acts 3:21)*. The devil is required to restore everything he stole from us. God is in the process of restoring everything that was affected by the fall.

6. TRANSFORMATION

This is a dramatic outward change by manifesting the new man or the new creation within *(2 Corinthians 5:17, 3:18; Romans 12:2)*.

The Bible says that if anyone is in Christ, he is a new creation. New creations cannot have old DNA. We have received new DNA through our new birth. To manifest the nature of that new creation, we need to go through transformation by renewing our mind daily with the Word of God.

DISCOVERING THE LOST KINGDOM

MANIFESTATION

Through this, we reveal kingdom sonship to the creation around us, manifesting the image and likeness of God, which is our true identity *(Romans 8:9; 1 Corinthians 12:7)*. All of creation is waiting for the manifestation of the sons of God. It is groaning with birth pangs, waiting to be set free from the corruption that came upon it with our fall.

Through salvation, God restored everything we lost, but that is not what we have been taught. Let me show you from the Scriptures that what I am saying is true.

- Sonship *(John 1:12; Romans 8:15–17; Galatians 4:5; 1 John 3:1)*
- Dominion over the Earth *(Matthew 5:5; Matthew 28:18–19; Mark 16:16–19; Luke 10:19; Acts 1:8)*
- Provision and Shelter *(Matthew 6:9–11, 33)*
- Glory of God *(John 17:22; 2 Corinthians 3:18; Hebrews 2:10)*
- Kingdom of God *(Luke 12:32, 22:29; Matthew 6:33; Mark 9:1)*
- Purpose *(Matthew 5:5; 1 Corinthians 4:8;*
- *Revelation 1:6, 5:9–10, 22:5)*
- God's Spirit *(Acts 2:17; John 14:16–17; Romans 8:11)*
- The Tree of Life *(Revelation 22:1-2)*

All relationships that were broken or became out of order because of the fall were reconciled or put back in the right order on the cross, through Jesus Christ.

THE PROCESS OF SALVATION

- Relationship between man and God *(Romans 5:1, 10; Romans 8:15; 2 Corinthians 5:18)*

- Relationship between heaven and earth *(Ephesians 1:10; Colossians 1:20)*

- Relationship between man and nature *(Mark 16:15; Romans 8:19–22)*

- Relationship within mankind *(John 4:23–24; Philippians 3:3; 1 Thessalonians 5:23)*

- Relationship with fellow humans *(Romans 3:29; 1 Corinthians 12:13)*

- Relationship with the demonic world *(Luke 10:19; John 12:31, 16:11; Colossians 2:15)*

Please read and study the above Bible verses and make them a part of your belief system.

This is why all the major doctrines and kingdom concepts in the New Testament start with the prefix "RE," which means to do something again. Following are thirteen of those concepts and doctrines.

- **Re**pent *(Matthew 4:17)*
- **Re**turn *(1 Peter 2:25)*
- **Re**storation *(Acts 3:21)*
- **Re**deem *(Galatians 4:4-5)*
- **Re**new *(Romans 12:2)*
- **Re**birth *(John 3:3)*
- **Re**ceive *(John 20:22)*
- **Re**conciliation *(2 Corinthians 5:18)*

DISCOVERING THE LOST KINGDOM

- **Re**stitution *(Acts 3:21)*
- **Re**generation *(Titus 3:4-6)*
- **Re**lease *(Hebrews 2:14-15)*
- **Re**cover *(Mark 16:18; Luke 4:18*
- **Re**ward *(Colossians 3:24; Revelation 22:12)*
- **Re**surrection *(1 Corinthians 15:13&21)*

Once we are saved, we are supposed to go back to God's original intent for us.

The moment you meet Jesus, you are supposed to be propelled into your purpose and calling. That's what happened to the disciples and Paul when they met Him. Anyone who had an encounter with God (Moses, Gideon, etc.) was released to walk in their calling. If we do not, it means we have a wrong understanding about the salvation we received, and we might have met a religious Jesus rather than the true Jesus *(2 Corinthians 11:4)*. There are many Jesuses and different spirits that are not from God.

If a person received the real Jesus of the Bible and the true Holy Spirit, they should have a sense of purpose and revelation of the kingdom of their Father. Otherwise, what they received is not the true Jesus and His Spirit.

Many are deceived by the religious spirit and think they are saved just to go to heaven. Notice that heaven, worship, and religion are not included in the above list of things we lost when Adam fell. Adam did not fall from heaven; he did not lose heaven when he fell. He lost his birthright and the dominion and rule of the earth. God decided to restore what we lost through the process of salvation. This is very important to understand.

THE PROCESS OF SALVATION

God sent His Son, Jesus Christ, who is called the Last Adam *(1 Corinthians 15:45)*, to die for our sins and to save us from everything the fall and sin brought upon us. Once you're saved, you are supposed to be free from the consequences of the fall. Otherwise, the process of salvation is not yet complete.

Through salvation, God restored to us everything we lost. Whoever believes in Jesus, God gave them the authority to become a child of God *(John 1:12; 1 John 3:1)*.

Jesus said that if we seek His kingdom and righteousness first, then all the provision we need will be added to us *(Matthew 6:33; Luke 12:30–31)*.

Everything Jesus did was to show us how to have dominion over the earth. Whether He walked on water, calmed the storm, gave a miraculous catch of fish, healed the sick, or cast out demons, He provided examples of how humans are supposed to live on the earth.

Jesus called Himself the Son of man. He was showing us how we are supposed to live through His life. We have the same nature, authority, and ownership as Jesus; we are joint heirs with Him *(Romans 8:16–17)*.

The whole reason for salvation is to restore us and the earth to our original state and purpose.

When the children of God are liberated, all of creation will be delivered from the bondage of corruption *(Romans 8:19–21)*. The blood of Jesus is sufficient to reverse and restore all of the damage that was caused by the fall of Adam. How many people believe that today?

DISCOVERING THE LOST KINGDOM

THE NEED FOR ANOTHER GARDEN

There arose the need for another garden, person, gate, or nation for God to operate through to govern His kingdom on earth. When man is restored to his original intent, he needs a command center or place of operation to establish God's kingdom and will on earth. This new garden is not called the garden of Eden like in Genesis. It is called the *Ekklesia*, or what we call the *church*. The church is the garden of God through which He accomplishes His will and plan on earth right now *(1 Corinthians 3:9)*.

In the beginning, God planted the garden and put the man in it. In the New Testament, He put the garden (kingdom) inside of us and then releases us to manifest it through the specific calling each one of us has. Every human carries the kingdom garden in their spirit man. That is why Jesus told the Pharisees that the kingdom of God is within them. *(Luke 17:20-21)*.

How did the kingdom get inside the Pharisees? They were not born again or Spirit-filled, but they were born with it. Since the kingdom of God is within each human, the kind of kingdom they manifest depends on which spirit world each one is connected to. If a person is connected to the demonic world, the kingdom they manifest will be the kingdom of darkness.

When we are saved, at least some dimension of the life Adam (we were in Adam) once had in Eden should manifest in our lives. If the sin and fall of Adam could affect the entire human race regardless of our choice, then once we are saved, we should be able to tap into the life Adam had before the fall. Adam didn't have to sing in order for God to manifest in the garden; he had a Father-son relationship with God Almighty. That is the kind of relationship He always wanted with humans, though it was broken for a while because of our

THE PROCESS OF SALVATION

disobedience (Exodus 4:22; Deuteronomy 32:18; 2 Samuel 7:12–16; 2Corinthians 6:17–18).

That's why there was so much singing in the Old Testament after the fall; they didn't know how to relate to God as their Father. Sonship was not available to everyone, only to a select few. That concept was too foreign for them. They needed singing to create a dwelling place for God. It is very sad today that many saved and adopted children still struggle to relate to God as their Father. It is hard for them to believe God dwells in them and that they are His children and have access to His throne 24/7.

Many are still seeking God's presence through singing, without knowing that He is living in them every moment of every day. They talk about going into His presence and coming out of it. They have been programmed by religion for so long that it is hard for them to think anything different. Their theology is still based on the Old Testament. Everything they do in their services is based on pre-born-again concepts.

How did Jesus relate to His Father while He was on earth? How many songs did He sing before He could talk to Him? Show me one single reference from the New Testament, and then I will believe your theology. How did the disciples relate to Jesus? We should do the same. We should learn to relate to God our Father as Adam did before the fall and how Jesus did while He was on earth. That is His original design for us.

If you're having a hard time relating to God as your Father, I encourage you to be saved. It doesn't matter how long you have been in church. You may need some deliverance or counseling to receive healing from wounds you might have from your earthly father—wounds that are hindering you from knowing your heavenly Father.

How many of you had to sing four songs before you got to talk or share with your earthly father or for him to talk and share with you? Once we are saved, we enter into a Father- child relationship with God *(Matthew 6:9; John 1:12)*.

BECOMING A GATE OF HEAVEN

Each believer in Jesus Christ is a gate of heaven on earth right now. When you receive Christ, you become a dwelling place of God and a temple of the Holy Spirit (1 Corinthians 3:16, 6:19). Please don't just seek His presence: seek Him. You have a direct connection with heaven (Romans 5:2; Ephesians 2:18). You have been chosen by God to release and execute His will and purpose.

The purpose of a gate is to give or deny access. When we become the gate of heaven on earth, we give access to God to accomplish His will. In order to do that, we need to come into full alignment with God and heaven.

Humans are the only species that has the legal right to allow or forbid anything on earth *(Matthew 16:19)*. That is the way God works in partnership with us.

In the Old Testament, the gate of heaven was a physical place. First, it was the garden of Eden. When Jacob left his house to go to Padan Aram, his mother's place, on the way he reached a place called Luz and slept there. During the night, he had a dream, and God spoke to him in the dream. He saw a ladder that was set up between the earth and heaven, and the angels of God were ascending and descending on it.

When Jacob woke up, he realized God was in that place, so he called the name of the city Bethel, which means "the house of God" or "the gate of heaven."

THE PROCESS OF SALVATION

> *And he was afraid and said, "How awesome is this place! This is none other than the house of God, and this is the gate of heaven!" (Genesis 28:17)*

In the New Testament, it's not a building or a place that is called a house or gate of heaven, but a person.

> *Jesus answered and said to him, "Because I said to you, 'I saw you under the fig tree,' do you believe? You will see greater things than these." And He said to him, "Most assuredly, I say to you, hereafter you shall see heaven open, and the angels of God ascending and descending upon the Son of Man."(John 1:50–51)*

Jesus is the gate of heaven because He is the Son of God. Whoever believes in Him and receives Him becomes a child of God, and in turn, becomes a gate of heaven or the garden of God on earth. To become a gate of heaven, a person needs to become a house of God. House of God means a place where God dwells. Where does God dwell now? Though He is in heaven, He dwells in each believer through His Spirit.

We are called a house of God in the New Testament (Ephesians 2:22). He also dwells in His church. In the Old Testament, the temple—or the house of God—was a building made of hands. In the New Testament, the temple—or the house of God—is made up of the people who receive Jesus into their lives (John 2:19, 21; 1 Corinthians 3:16–17, 6:19), and not a building.

Keep in mind that the church is not a building. The church is not a physical building made of bricks and iron. It is a building made of living stones, which are believers who are saved and washed by the blood of Jesus *(1 Peter 2:5)*.

> **But if I am delayed, I write so that you may know how you ought to conduct yourself in the house of God, which is the church of the living God, the pillar and ground of the truth. (1 Timothy 3:15)**

As a church, we are being built as the dwelling place for God. If we are the dwelling place of God, then we don't need to create another alternative or temporary dwelling for God through our singing. People say and do that because of the lack of understanding about New Testament theology and the doctrine of God.

> **In whom the whole building, being fitted together, grows into a holy temple in the Lord, in whom you also are being built together for a dwelling place of God in the Spirit. (Ephesians 2:21-22)**

We need to become the house of God or the gate of heaven in order to release and execute God's kingdom purposes on earth and to identify and destroy the gates of hell and their works, as Jesus said in Matthew 16:18. In other words, we become a gate of heaven to give God access to operate on earth and to deny access to Satan, and his demons, to keep them from accomplishing his will here.

CHAPTER 6

WHY IS THE MESSAGE OF THE KINGDOM SO VITAL

I must preach the kingdom of God to the other cities also, because for this purpose I have been sent. (Luke 4:43)

Why is the message of the kingdom so vitally important to the body of Christ and the world? Because Jesus's top priority is His kingdom. He preached and taught about it more than any other subject.

As you read in the previous chapter, we were created to live in Eden. Eden was the extension of God's kingdom on earth. God's will was done in Eden as it was in heaven. There is no sickness, poverty, curse, or death in heaven, and there was no sickness, poverty, curse, or death in Eden. Adam was not created to die.

He was an eternal spirit-being created in the image and likeness of God to administer His kingdom on earth. God never mentioned anything about worship or going to heaven to Adam and Eve. They were created to live and reign on earth forever and ever. That is why the first and last chapters of the Bible say the same thing about the purpose of man *(See Genesis 1:26 and Revelation 22:5).* We were created to reign on the earth.

The enemy deceived Adam and Eve. They fell from their position and from their relationship with God, and creation came under bondage because of it. They did not fall from heaven; instead, they fell from a position of governance and were cast out of Eden. Man lost the kingdom of God and began to live on earth without it.

The enemy established a counterfeit kingdom (Babylonian System) and took man further away from God, luring him with things that satisfied his flesh, namely control (false power) and independence (false freedom).

We have been like kidnapped children, with our captor trying to pacify us and make us happy by giving us toys and candies and everything else our flesh wants. Outwardly, we show that we are happy, but in the spirit, we feel unfulfilled and long to be back home with our Daddy. We are all looking for our homeland.

THE GOSPEL OF THE KINGDOM

What is the gospel of the kingdom? Gospel simply means good news. The gospel of the kingdom means the good news of the kingdom. God is King and He has a kingdom that He wants to see established on the earth.

The kingdom man lost has been restored. That is the simple definition of the gospel of the kingdom. That is the good news of the kingdom Jesus came to announce.

God did not give up on us. He wanted to reinstate us to our original position and restore His kingdom back to us. He knows that we cannot live fulfilled on earth without His kingdom. God sent His Son, Jesus Christ, with the message of the kingdom and its imminent

WHY IS THE MESSAGE OF THE KINGDOM SO VITAL

return to earth. Since the time Adam lost it, our spirits have been yearning for our homeland. Everyone on earth since Adam has been looking for a better place to live—for a better country and for a better government. We misinterpreted it as waiting to go to heaven or migrating into some developed countries.

In the Bible days, people longed to go to Egypt and live there because it was a prosperous and more developed nation than others at that time. Even Jacob sent his children there to buy food during famine. In our time, people from developing countries long to immigrate to a developed country for better living and employment. People from the developed countries long to be at some vacation spot or resort. It's a universal thing for which every heart yearns.

All believers who have not yet discovered the kingdom of God, regardless of how long they have been saved and Spirit-filled, will sense there is something missing. They are longing for something just out of their reach, something more for them somewhere. Many interpret this feeling as a hunger for more of God or for His Spirit, or to migrate to a more developed country or better community; but in truth, their spirit is longing for the homeland they lost. Others misinterpret it as a longing for revival or the rapture.

Everyone who lived during the Old Testament time longed for a country too. Even though they were used by God and fulfilled their calling, there was a longing in their spirit for a better country or city whose Maker and Builder was God *(Hebrews 11:10)*. They were longing for the kingdom of God, which their forefather Adam lost. But it was not made available to them. That is why the Bible says in Hebrews 11:

> **These all died in faith, not having received the promises, but having seen them afar off were assured of**

> **them, embraced them and confessed that they were strangers and pilgrims on the earth. For those who say such things declare plainly that they seek a home-land. And truly if they had called to mind that country from which they had come out, they would have had opportunity to return. But now they desire a better, that is, a heavenly country. Therefore God is not ashamed to be called their God, for He has prepared a city for them. (Hebrews 11:13–16)**

These verses are powerful and reveal a hidden truth. Though I read this many times, I never understood what it really meant. It is extremely important to notice that these people in the Old Testament were not longing for more of God, more of His Spirit, or revival.

They were all longing for a country, or as quoted above, a homeland.

Notice the sentence, "If they had called to mind that country from which they had come out, they would have had opportunity to return." To what country were they longing to return? This refers to the heavenly country (kingdom of God) they came from, out of which their forefather Adam came. When Adam came out of the kingdom (garden) of God, we all left the kingdom with him. Since then, we have been longing to return to the kingdom of God. Why were they looking for a country and not for God? As I said earlier, we are created to live in God's kingdom. Until we discover it, we will not be satisfied.

They were all looking for a heavenly country, the kingdom of God, which was revealed in the New Testament with the coming of Jesus Christ. "Heavenly country" is another reference to the kingdom of heaven.

WHY IS THE MESSAGE OF THE KINGDOM SO VITAL

None of the Old Testament believers had the opportunity to hear the message of the kingdom, or the opportunity to live in it as we do today. That is why Jesus said in Matthew 13:17, "for assuredly, I say to you that many prophets and righteous men desired to see what you see, and did not see it, and to hear what you hear, and did not hear it." What is Jesus talking about? He is not talking about miracles, but seeing and hearing the message of the kingdom of God. There were plenty of miracles in the Old Testament times.

The time finally came when God decided to restore the kingdom to us. He sent His Son, Jesus, to reveal and teach us about it and show us how to live in it. That is why Jesus preached the kingdom of God more than any other subject. It was the first and last message He preached *(Matthew 4:17; Acts 1:3)*.

> **Now after John was put in prison, Jesus came to Galilee, preaching the gospel of the kingdom of God, and saying, "The time is fulfilled, and the kingdom of God is at hand. Repent, and believe in the gospel." (Mark 1:14–15)**

Jesus was saying that the time is fulfilled for the kingdom of God to be restored to man. Jesus came to announce the imminent arrival of the kingdom of God to the earth. That is why He said, "The kingdom is at hand." "At hand" means near, not two thousand years away.

The reason the phrase kingdom of heaven appears only in the gospel of Matthew is because it is the first book of the New Testament and it is announcing the reentry of this heavenly country to planet Earth *(Matthew 4:17; Mark 1:14–15)*. Jesus came with a kingdom, or a country; His pivotal message was not taking us to heaven but bringing heaven to us.

He said in Luke 12:32, "Do not fear, little flock, for it is your Father's good pleasure to give you the kingdom." He did not come to give us a church or a particular denomination, but the very kingdom *(Luke 22:29)*.

Jesus began His preaching by announcing, "Repent, for the kingdom of heaven is at hand" *(Matthew 4:17b)*. What He meant by it is this: The country that all the people on earth, especially the Old Testament saints, were longing to see and live in is at hand. It's almost here. Wow! What good news! The gospel is called good news, and sadly, we have turned it into a religion.

In the New Testament, we read that believers were longing for a better city, not a country. We received the country already through Jesus, but not the city yet. Which city are we seeking? The New Jerusalem, which will come down from heaven; the capital city of the kingdom of God on earth is what we should be longing for as well.

> ***But now they desire a better, that is, a heavenly country. Therefore God is not ashamed to be called their God, for He has prepared a city for them. (Hebrews 11:16)***

> ***For here we have no continuing city, but we seek the one to come. (Hebrews 13:14)***

The Jews wrote the above verses. They were living (or had lived) in Israel at some point and had been to the natural city of Jerusalem. But the above verses say they were still longing for another city that was yet to come. Which city are they talking about? Most Christians from around the world desire to visit Israel and the old city of Jerusalem, but the people who were living in Jerusalem were longing to be in some other city. Isn't that ironic? They were not longing for the natural city of Jerusalem, but the heavenly one, the New Jerusalem.

> ***He who overcomes, I will make him a pillar in the temple of My God, and he shall go out no more. I will write on***

WHY IS THE MESSAGE OF THE KINGDOM SO VITAL

him the name of My God and the name of the city of My God, the New Jerusalem, which comes down out of heaven from My God. And I will write on him My new name. (Revelation 3:12)

Then I, John, saw the holy city, New Jerusalem, coming down out of heaven from God, prepared as a bride adorned for her husband. (Revelation 21:2)

In the secular world, people define this longing for an imaginary country called utopia: a land that is beautiful and plentiful, where there is no sorrow or worry. Every human is born with that instinct. That search will only end when each person comes to Christ and discovers the kingdom of God. We have been preaching wrongly all these years. We told people that only Jesus can fill the gap and longing in a person's soul. That is not complete. People who have Jesus are still longing for something more. It's not a person they are looking for, but a country. Only the kingdom of God can fill that vacuum in us.

In Hebrews 12:22, the writer tells us that we have already come to Mount Zion and the heavenly Jerusalem. "But you have come to Mount Zion and to the city of the living God, the heavenly Jerusalem, to an innumerable company of angels." Because of our religious background, it's hard for us to receive such biblical truths.

We are not taught about the finished work of Christ, but about a religion that never satisfies, no matter how much we do.

Many believers wait all their lives to die and go to heaven because they interpret the longing in their heart as a desire to go to heaven. Instead of discovering God's kingdom on earth and fulfilling His purpose here, they waste a lifetime just waiting. The religious gospel has trained us to think that once you are saved, your next stop is heaven.

> *The law and the prophets were until John. Since that time the kingdom of God has been preached, and everyone is pressing into it. (Luke 16:16)*

Why is everyone pressing in to get into the kingdom of God? When we preach our religious gospel of going to heaven, why do only a handful get saved? Because man is looking for a lost kingdom. When their spirit hears the announcement of the kingdom of God, they will run to get into it.

Unfortunately, instead of preaching the kingdom, many still preach the law and the prophets. Every time we preach the law and the prophets, we give people an outdated or expired system or meal. As a result, instead of people getting better, they go deeper into bondage. Why are people not pressing into the kingdom these days? Because they hear the wrong message. Many preach Moses and Elijah and think they are preaching the kingdom.

7 DIMENSIONS OF THE KINGDOM OF GOD

When we study in detail what Jesus came to reveal about the kingdom of God, we see that there are seven different dimensions He mentioned in the New Testament. I would like to explain each one of them in a nutshell.

1. JESUS BEGAN HIS MINISTRY BY ANNOUNCING THAT THE KINGDOM IS NEAR OR AT HAND

> *From that time Jesus began to preach and to say, "Repent, for the kingdom of heaven is at hand." (Matthew 4:17)*

That is the first dimension we see in the New Testament. Jesus and John the Baptist came announcing the same thing *(Matthew 3:2)*. They both announced the re-entry of the dimension of the kingdom

WHY IS THE MESSAGE OF THE KINGDOM SO VITAL

of God that was lifted from the earth when Adam was kicked out of the garden. That doesn't mean His kingdom was totally absent from the earth.

2. THE KINGDOM OF GOD THAT IS WITHIN US

> *Now when He was asked by the Pharisees when the kingdom of God would come, He answered them and said, "The kingdom of God does not come with observation; nor will they say, 'See here!' or 'See there!' For indeed, the kingdom of God is within you." (Luke 17:20-21)*

There is a dimension of the kingdom that is within each human being. We are kingdom builders by design.

The kind of kingdom that manifests on the earth through us depends on which spirit world each one of us is connected to.

The kingdom of God is an invisible kingdom; we cannot see it with our natural eyes *(Mark 4:26-29)*. God put His kingdom inside of us, and it manifests to the world through the work each one of us is called to do. It is God's desire that His will is done on this earth as it is in heaven. This can only be done through human beings because the earth was given to us.

The new era of the kingdom of God began to operate with the coming of the Holy Spirit on the day of Pentecost. The Ekklesia of Jesus's kingdom began to operate from that day onward.

The church has the same mission that God gave to Adam and to the nation of Israel *(Matthew 16:18-19)*. The church's primary purpose is to see God's will accomplished on earth as it is in heaven. That is what Jesus meant by telling us to go and disciple nations by going into the world *(Matthew 28:19; Mark 16:15)*.

3. THE KINGDOM THAT WE SEE WHEN WE ARE BORN AGAIN

> *Jesus answered and said to him, "Most assuredly, I say to you, unless one is born again, he cannot see the kingdom of God." (John 3:3)*

According to Jesus, when we are born again, we are supposed to see the kingdom of God. The kingdom that we see in the spirit is the aspect of the kingdom God wants to manifest through each one of us. It varies from person to person which aspect of the kingdom they were created to manifest. The first result of the born-again experience is the ability to see the kingdom of God that is within us, with the eyes of our spirit.

4. THE KINGDOM THAT IS HIDDEN IN THE WORLD

> *"Again, the kingdom of heaven is like treasure hidden in a field, which a man found and hid; and for joy over it he goes and sells all that he has and buys that field. (Matthew 13:44)*

There is a dimension of the kingdom of God that is hidden in the world today because the world was created by Jesus for His kingdom *(John 1:10)*. The enemy stole it from us and used the systems of this world to establish his kingdom. God wants to redeem and save it *(John 3:17)*.

Though the kingdom of God is in operation on earth, not everyone will find it because it is like treasure hidden in a field. Treasure is not easy to find, and only those who are very serious and willing to risk their lives will find it.

In the above parable, the *field* is the world, and the *treasure* is the kingdom of heaven *(Matthew 13:38)*. It is hidden, and God wants us to seek it. In another parable, Jesus compared the kingdom of heaven to a pearl of great price:

> **Again, the kingdom of heaven is like a merchant seeking beautiful pearls, who, when he had found one pearl of great price, went and sold all that he had and bought it. (Matthew 13:45–46)**

5. THE KINGDOM OF GOD THAT IS UPON US

> **But if I cast out demons with the finger of God, surely the kingdom of God has come upon you. (Luke 11:20)**

The finger of God in the Bible speaks of the Holy Spirit. Jesus was filled with the Holy Spirit, and wherever He went, He healed those who were oppressed of the devil *(Acts 10:38)*. When the kingdom of God manifests, demons have to flee.

The Holy Spirit comes with the kingdom of God. He comes to make it real to us and manifest it in the natural. That means that wherever the activities of the Holy Spirit are manifest, the kingdom of God is there. At present, without the Holy Spirit, no operation of the kingdom of God will ever be made manifest. But it doesn't mean that all we do is cast out demons by the Holy Spirit. Most people limit and know Him only for His gifts. He is much bigger than that.

Why don't we see the outpouring and the manifestation of the Holy Spirit as we saw in the first century? Many are asking and waiting for the outpouring of the Holy Spirit. He will be poured out only on people who are ready to establish and execute God's kingdom purpose on the earth.

That is why Jesus had to preach and teach about the kingdom of God for three years before the Father poured out the Holy Spirit.

He was not given so that we can feel good or have an emotional experience. He is the Governor of the kingdom, and He comes to accomplish the will of the King who sent Him. If we want to see Him in operation as we see in the book of Acts, then we need to preach what they preached and prepare the people.

Otherwise, it doesn't matter what program we have or how long we cry or shout; He will not manifest.

Do a study on the work of the Holy Spirit from Genesis to Revelation. He does everything God Himself does because He is God. When a person or a place becomes fully yielded to the Spirit of God, the kingdom of God will manifest and be in full operation there.

When a group of people are hungry and ready to manifest the kingdom, God will pour out His Spirit upon them.

6. THE KINGDOM OF GOD THAT CAME ON THE DAY OF PENTECOST

> *Jesus said, "Verily I say unto you, that there be some of them that stand here, which shall not taste of death, till they have seen the kingdom of God come with power." (Mark 9:1 KJV)*
>
> *Assuredly, I say to you, there are some standing here who shall not taste death till they see the Son of Man coming in His kingdom." (Matthew 16:28)*
>
> *But I tell you truly, there are some standing here who shall not taste death till they see the kingdom of God." (Luke 9:27)*

The kingdom that was lifted from the earth when Adam fell was restored to us on the day of Pentecost. This is the dimension of the kingdom that John the Baptist and Jesus came announcing. When the Holy Spirit comes to dwell in us, He comes with the kingdom of God. The kingdom of God is righteousness, peace, and joy in the Holy Spirit *(Romans 14:17)*. Wherever the Holy Spirit is, there is the kingdom of God.

The above verses in all of the Gospels are a turning point in the New Testament. What was Jesus talking about? If He was referring to His second coming, it would not be true. There is no way some people who were alive then would remain alive until His second coming. That would be impossible because people do not live that long. He was talking about the day of Pentecost when the Holy Spirit came with power.

Since that day, the kingdom of God began to operate on earth once again. That is what He meant when He said, "The kingdom of heaven is at hand." Many who had heard Jesus were alive to see it with their own eyes.

Nowhere in the book of Acts do we see any of the apostles preaching the kingdom-at-hand message. With the coming of the Holy Spirit in Acts 2, the kingdom of God arrived on earth, and it has been operating here ever since. Does everyone see and experience it? No. Why? Because it does not come with observation, but a born-again believer can see it with his or her spiritual eyes.

This is the dimension of the kingdom that Jesus told us to pray for in the kingdom prayer He taught in Matthew 6:9-13. We don't see anyone praying this prayer after the day of Pentecost.

7. THE KINGDOM OF GOD AS A COUNTRY

> *Your kingdom come. Your will be done on earth as it is in heaven. (Matthew 6:10)*

DISCOVERING THE LOST KINGDOM

"For the kingdom of heaven is like a man traveling to a far country, who called his own servants and delivered his goods to them. (Matthew 25:14)

The seventh dimension revealed in the Gospels is the kingdom of God as a country. God wants to invade the earth with His kingdom. The kingdom of heaven is a country. He wants to colonize the earth with His kingdom.

In the Gospels, we see progress in the parables Jesus shared about His kingdom. He started sharing it as a seed, and then toward the end of His ministry, He did not share it as a seed anymore but as a country. From a seed to a country, that's the pattern He gave us to follow. The kingdom always starts as a seed in a person's life or in a nation. In Matthew 13 alone, Jesus shared three parables about the kingdom of God being a seed *(Matthew 13:3-9; 19, 24, 31)*. Then in Matthew 25, 26, and in Luke 19, He shared three other parables to show His kingdom is an actual country *(Matthew 25:14; 25:34; 26:29; Luke 19:12-27)*.

Don't stop at the kingdom being only a seed. We need to sow it and nurture it until it becomes a country and fills our nations, and eventually, the whole earth *(Daniel 2:35)*. Until the kingdoms of this world become the kingdoms of our Lord and of His Christ *(Revelation 11:15)*. I have a whole book called 7 Dimensions and Operations of the Kingdom of God, which will greatly bless you.

When each of the above-mentioned dimensions of the kingdom of God manifest, it brings different results. We have been stuck with mainly one dimension and result, which is the power of God to cast out demons, save souls, heal the sick, and prophesy. Nobody taught us about the other dimensions.

WHY IS THE MESSAGE OF THE KINGDOM SO VITAL

The ultimate goal of the manifestation of all these dimensions is national transformation, or what the Bible calls "discipling nations." The kingdom starts as a seed, or leaven, then it grows. Seeds grow vertically, and leaven expands horizontally. This is an important principle to understand about how the kingdom grows in us and on the earth. It has to grow both vertically and horizontally until it fills the whole earth.

It starts with the transformation of the person who received the message of the kingdom. It starts as a seed inside that person and gradually takes over that person: everything he or she does and how they think.

Once we are transformed, we can't remain the same and continue to do the same old religious things or the things of Babylon. You will feel like you don't fit in the old system anymore, and the sooner you can come out of it, the better your life will be. But there is a great battle involved in all this process.

When Jesus came announcing the imminent arrival of the kingdom, what preceded that dimension were signs, wonders, and miracles. Each individual is uniquely created to manifest a particular aspect of the kingdom of God. That is the dimension that is within us. The third dimension is seeing the kingdom that is within us when we are born again.

This world was designed and created by Jesus as a place to establish His kingdom. But what we see now in the world are duplicates or pseudo entities, whether it is government, media, or education. The real ones are of the kingdom of God. When the kingdoms of this world become the kingdoms of our Lord, everything that is false will pass away.

When the kingdom of God comes upon a person, the result will be deliverance from demonic possession and strongholds, and from the bondages and traditions of the culture they grew up in. This is the result of the fifth dimension of the kingdom when it manifests.

When the Holy Spirit came on the day of Pentecost, a new dimension of the kingdom arrived: the dimension that Jesus and John the Baptist announced. That day, the governing body of the kingdom, Ekklesia (church), was birthed, which is supposed to disciple nations until the seventh dimension of the kingdom is manifested in the nations of the world.

Each one of us is created to manifest one of the dimensions of the kingdom of God on the earth or be a part of it. We can't do by ourselves what He has called us to do. When the entire human race manifests the seven dimensions of the kingdom on earth, the whole earth will be transformed and filled with the glory of God as the waters cover the sea.

When you discover the kingdom of God, the longing of your heart and spirit for a place or country will cease; for the very first time you will feel in your spirit that you are finally home. Until you discover it, nothing else will satisfy you, no matter how rich or poor you are or how long you have been Spirit- filled or in ministry. Instead of seeking first God's kingdom, which Jesus told us to do, believers today keep going from one revival meeting to another and from one conference to the next, being robbed and taken advantage of by so-called ministers.

GRACE AND THE KINGDOM

We must seek His kingdom with everything we have until we discover it. In Hebrews, the author concludes by saying:

> ***Therefore, since we are receiving a kingdom which cannot be shaken, let us have grace. (Hebrews 12:28)***

WHY IS THE MESSAGE OF THE KINGDOM SO VITAL

Many go after the teaching of grace these days, too. The trouble is that before we can gain it, we must first have a revelation of the kingdom of God. The above verse says we will have grace after we receive a kingdom that cannot be shaken, because grace is the operating system of the kingdom of God. The kingdom is the country, and grace is the system of governing.

In His kingdom, God deals with us through His grace. In computer terms, the kingdom is the hardware and grace is the software. What good is having the most powerful software in the world with no hardware to operate it? How does that benefit anyone?

Every nation has a political or governing system. For example, India is democratic, and China has a communist government. The kingdom of God is a nation ruled by a King, who is God, and He uses grace as His governing system. Before we go after grace, we need to discover His kingdom. That is why Jesus told us to seek first the kingdom and not grace.

God's children need the same environment, like Eden, to survive. We won't go back into a physical Eden; instead, He put Eden (the kingdom) inside of us *(Luke 17:20–21)*. When God created man and put him on earth, He established a process, or a political system, to take care of man. That system is called the kingdom of God, which is the same system He has in heaven.

MISUNDERSTANDINGS ABOUT THE KINGDOM

When Jesus preached the kingdom of God, He met the physical needs of the people first. He healed their sickness and promised them that if they sought His kingdom first, their food, clothing, and the basic things of life would be provided. For many years, I thought there was no food or drink in the kingdom of God because God's kingdom is spiritual.

DISCOVERING THE LOST KINGDOM

I only understood the religious side of spirituality and not the kingdom side. We tend to separate things in life as spiritual and secular. In the garden, everything was spiritual. Even taking care of the trees and having dominion was equally spiritual to Adam meeting with God in the cool of the day.

The reason Jesus healed and delivered the people was to show us that those sicknesses and bondages did not belong to His kingdom. They came from another kingdom. He was evicting or casting out from people those things that He did not give and were not of His kingdom. He also taught them to reveal the lies that people believed about themselves, God, and His kingdom. There are eight major misunderstandings about the kingdom of God.

1. **Miracles and healing are kingdom:** Many think that healing the sick and doing miracles is the kingdom of God. They are not the kingdom, just signs of the kingdom. When you go to a place or a location, you will see the signs long before you reach your destination. Those signs lead you or tell you about the place you want to go. Jesus sent His disciples to heal the sick, to cleanse the lepers, to raise the dead, and then tell them that the kingdom of God is near, or at hand. That means those miracles were not the kingdom, but the signs that it was about to arrive *(Matthew 10:7–8; Luke 10:9)*.

2. **God's kingdom cannot be on the earth:** Jesus said, "My kingdom is not of this world" (John 18:36a). I thought there couldn't be anything material in His kingdom because it is not of this world, but that is not what Jesus meant. He meant that His kingdom is not like the kingdoms of this world because it is not from here. He never said His kingdom is not in this world.

In the kingdoms of this world, rulers abuse and oppress the citizens, and the king's servants fight for the king to protect him. They tax

WHY IS THE MESSAGE OF THE KINGDOM SO VITAL

people to pay for what the king needs. Initially, they will promise them good things, but eventually, they will rob and kill them. Jesus was saying, My kingdom is not like that. I don't tax people to pay for My needs. *My kingdom is self-sufficient and feeds the whole world. In My kingdom, I fight to protect the people. I didn't come to be served, but to serve, and to give My life as a ransom for many.*

Jesus told His disciples:

> **Not everyone who says to Me, "Lord, Lord," shall enter the kingdom of heaven, but he who does the will of My Father in heaven. Many will say to Me in that day, "Lord, Lord, have we not prophesied in Your name, cast out demons in Your name, and done many wonders in Your name?" And then I will declare to them, "I never knew you; depart from Me, you who practice lawlessness!" (Matthew 7:21–23)**

We have been taught that the kingdom of God is all about healing, prophesying, helping the poor, and casting out demons. In the above verses, Jesus is saying that you can do all those things and still miss the will of God for your life and His kingdom. That astounds me! If casting out demons and healing the sick, prophesying, and doing many wonders are not His will, then what is the will of our heavenly Father? We live in a world where many believers run after miracles and prophetic words.

Don't misunderstand me. I am not against miracles, healing, prophesying, or wonders. They have their place in the kingdom. Most of the healings that take place today are for the believers in the church, but they are supposed to be signs for the unbelievers, and we are supposed to be living in divine health and provision. You may ask, "Then what is God's will?" He revealed that in the prayer

He taught His disciples: for His kingdom to come and His will to be done on earth as it is in heaven.

3. **There is no food or anything material in God's kingdom:** Many people quote the verse from Romans 14:17 that says the kingdom of God isn't about eating and drinking but righteousness, peace, and joy in the Holy Spirit. I once thought that there was nothing to eat in the kingdom of God and that we will fast every day if we are in God's kingdom.

That is far from the truth! In fact, Jesus said, "But I say to you, I will not drink of this fruit of the vine from now on until that day when I drink it new with you in My Father's kingdom" *(Matthew 26:29)*. Jesus also ate and drank with the disciples after His resurrection *(Acts 10:40–41; Luke 14:15)*.

There is definitely food and drink in God's kingdom. What Romans 14:17 means is the kingdom of God is not *made* of food and drink; though it most certainly has food and drink. In any kingdom, people have to eat in order to live. In fact, the first thing Jesus promised we would find when we discover the kingdom is food and other material things we need *(Matthew 6:33)*.

4. **Kingdom means going to church on Sundays:** For others, when they hear about the kingdom, they think about going to church. Church is not the kingdom, but *the church* is its governing body. Because of confusion and misunderstanding of the kingdom of God, we have been misinformed about the truth of the kingdom message Jesus and the apostles preached.

5. **The kingdom is only for the Jewish people:** Many believe the kingdom message was meant only for the Jewish people. That is a misconception. If it was only for the Jews, Jesus wouldn't have

taught us to pray for His kingdom to come and for His will to be done on earth as it is in heaven. Again, He said in Matthew 24:14 to preach the gospel of the kingdom in all the world— in every nation—as a witness. His kingdom is for the whole earth and every nation—not just Israel.

6. **The kingdom will only come during the millennial reign**: Another misunderstanding is that God's kingdom will come during the millennial reign of Christ on the earth. Until then, the kingdom is not available, and it won't manifest on the earth. Our number-one responsibility is to reveal Jesus and manifest His kingdom to people and creation. That's why Christ and His kingdom are inside of us.

7. **Seeking God's kingdom means doing ministry, getting baptized, or going to a Bible school:** In many religious circles, people believe that seeking God's kingdom means going out into the streets and doing some ministry, getting baptized and becoming a member of a particular church, or even going to a Bible school. That is far from the truth. Those are all religious interpretations of what Jesus meant when He told us to seek first His kingdom and His righteousness.

8. **The kingdom means getting closer to God:** Once we receive Jesus, He comes to live in us. How can we get closer to Someone who is already living inside of us? Our perception, paradigms, and understanding change based on the revelation we receive. Now that we understand what the kingdom of God is all about, let's see how we seek it. Jesus told us to seek it first before we seek anything else in life.

CHAPTER 7

SEEK THE KINGDOM FIRST

But seek first the kingdom of God and His righteousness, and all these things shall be added to you.
(Matthew 6:33)

Jesus told us to seek His kingdom first, not revival. People are seeking all kinds of things: relationships, money, job miracles, spiritual gifts, material things, success, fame—but nothing will satisfy them. Only the Creator knows the needs of His creation. When the Creator created us, He designed us in a way that we cannot live without a kingdom.

It is very important for you to know what the kingdom of God is before you start seeking it. Many people have fragmented ideas about the kingdom. A simple definition of a kingdom is a territory or a nation ruled by a king, where the king's will and plans are executed without question. In this case, God is the King. He has a country called heaven, and He wants to see His rule, or dominion, come to the earth.

DISCOVERING THE LOST KINGDOM

Many think of the kingdom of God futuristically—something that will take place later in time or as a place or state they will reach after they die.

How would you feel if someone said, "From today on, I will provide the food, shelter, and clothing for you and your family so that you can be free to do what you were born to do"? That is exactly what Jesus is saying by telling us to seek His kingdom first. Then all the things we need in life will be added to us.

Seeking God's kingdom does not mean getting baptized, reading the Bible, going to a Bible school, praying every day, sharing the gospel, or becoming a member of a church and speaking in tongues. The devil doesn't want you to discover God's kingdom.

He wants to keep you a slave in his kingdom, and to a religion called Christianity, until you die.

You can be saved and still not live in God's kingdom. According to Jesus, before we do anything spiritual or Christian, He wants us to seek His kingdom first. Now the questions are: What is God's kingdom? How do we seek it? The word kingdom refers to the dominion of a king. Jesus is the King and He has a kingdom. His children are supposed to live in His kingdom.

We are supposed to be seeking His dominion, or rule, in each area of our life. When an aspect of our life comes under the dominion or rule of Jesus, His kingdom has come and His will is done in that area of our life as it is in heaven. That is what He taught us to pray. Once our life comes under His dominion, then we can bring the same to the community we are living in, and eventually, to the whole nation.

When many people think of God's kingdom, they think it is all about power. Every kingdom has power, but that's not all a kingdom has.

SEEK THE KINGDOM FIRST

Some say it is righteousness, peace, and joy in the Holy Spirit. That is the culture of the kingdom. That's the culture we are supposed to be living in. Compare that culture with the culture you are living in right now, and notice the things people do to be happy, to have fun, and to have peace of mind!

The kingdom of God has an economy. We are supposed to live our lives based on kingdom economy, not the world's notions about money and success. Kingdom education is also different from the education system of the world. The world's education focuses on getting a degree and a job. Kingdom education focuses on discovering your purpose and calling and developing your gifts and skills.

A company can fire you from your job, but they cannot fire you from your purpose. An employer can remove you from your position, but he or she cannot take away your gifts and the skills you've developed.

Every person has at least one natural and spiritual gift. If we look at the lives of the disciples of Jesus, they were fishermen (or businessmen) before Jesus called them. That was their natural means of meeting their needs. After He called them, He gave them power and authority to heal the sick and cast out demons. That was their spiritual gift. Then He sent them out to do what He taught them to do. He said the worker is worthy of his food (*Matthew 10:10*). That is the kingdom pattern for receiving the provision we need.

The kingdom has a healthcare system, too. Do you know how many trillions of dollars our nation spends on healthcare? When kingdom healthcare comes, people live a healthy lifestyle. That healthy lifestyle protects their bodies from injury and builds their immune systems to fight disease and sickness. When you live in God's kingdom, He will show you what is good for you to eat and what to stay away from (Isaiah 55:2). There is no sickness in God's kingdom. The kingdom of God also has an agricultural system. We are not supposed to be eating what the world is producing, which is mostly poisonous and causes disease. The kingdom is supposed to have its own food production system.

The kingdom healthcare system is not about healing the sick, but teaching people how to live a healthy lifestyle. It is all about going back to the garden. In the garden, Adam was not living by miracles.

Jesus told us to seek His kingdom to free us. Many people do not feel free to do what they were born to do. They are stuck at a job they don't enjoy, but they are doing it to provide for their families.

WHY DID JESUS TELL US TO SEEK HIS KINGDOM FIRST?

1. MAN IS DESIGNED AND CREATED TO LIVE IN, AND BUILD, A KINGDOM

Without a kingdom, either the kingdom of God or the kingdom of darkness, we will not survive on this earth. We have a choice. It's up to us to live in and build God's kingdom. If we do not do that, we will build up the kingdom of darkness or our own little kingdoms instead.

In every man is the desire to design, govern, rule, build, establish, raise up, and accomplish something, or to help someone else do it. When a man cannot do that, he gets frustrated. And if something doesn't happen the way he planned while he is doing that, he wants to destroy it. If a man does not have that desire in him, something happened to his manhood and it needs to be restored. A woman is designed and created to help a man build a kingdom, to be the queen by his side. If a woman does not have that desire, then something happened to her womanhood and it needs to be restored. It is their natural instinct.

In the gospel of Luke, we read that when the kingdom of God was preached, everyone pressed in to be a part of it. It was like they had all been waiting for something but did not realize what it was they were waiting for until they heard the message of the kingdom. When they heard it, they recognized it and they ran to get inside.

> ***The law and the prophets were until John. Since that time the kingdom of God has been preached, and everyone is pressing into it. (Luke 16:16)***

Another verse says,

> ***And from the days of John the Baptist until now the kingdom of heaven suffers violence, and the violent take it by force. (Matthew 11:12)***

When the kingdom of God is being preached, the natural response of man should be, "Yes, I want it!" You do not have seek His kingdom first. As our Creator, He knows what worry does to the body and mind.

2. MAN IS WORRIED ABOUT HIS BASIC NEEDS

The majority of people spend most of their lives working a job to provide food, clothing, and shelter for themselves and their families. Naturally, people are worried about what they are going to eat and wear, and where they are going to live. Jesus said that's not the way life in His kingdom ought to be, or how His children are supposed to live. He said that food, clothing, and shelter will be added to His children as a result of them seeking His kingdom. In His kingdom, the King provides for His children so they can spend their precious time here doing what is really important, which is discovering and doing His will.

The precious and short time we have on earth is not to be wasted trying to make a living. Life is more important than finding food, clothing, and shelter. For many people, the most precious asset they have is their house, which will perish after a while. We are supposed to be working for what is eternal: His kingdom.

When we seek His kingdom, Jesus will provide our basic needs, which will free us up to spend all of our time doing what He created us to do. When all the people on earth discover His kingdom, there won't be a hunger problem.

3. JESUS KNOWS THE SIDE EFFECTS OF WORRY AND STRESS

Worry and stress are the root causes of many of the illnesses and diseases of the modern day. That is why Jesus said repeatedly not to worry about our life but to

4. MAN IS SEARCHING FOR A LOST COUNTRY

As I mentioned earlier, everyone on earth is looking for a better place to live and be happy. The human heart longs for the kingdom we lost with the fall of Adam. The kingdom of God is the only country that will fulfill that longing. That is why He told us to seek His kingdom first.

5. MAN IS LONGING FOR RIGHTEOUS GOVERNMENT

Every human is looking for a government to solve their problems, and to provide for, protect, and take care of them. Since we lost the kingdom of God, mankind has come up with different forms of government, and none of them has worked yet to solve our problems. Kingdoms of men, democracy, socialism, communism, and capitalism are some examples. We get tired of the unfulfilled promises our politicians make, and we elect a new government every few years.

We know in our heart that there is a perfect form of government somewhere out there that will work. There is only one perfect government that will fulfill the needs of mankind, and that is the government of God. That is why Scripture states that the government shall be upon His shoulders *(Isaiah 9:6)*, referring to Jesus. He came to this earth with a government and told us to seek it first.

6. SOCIAL AND RACIAL PROBLEMS WILL BE SOLVED

All over the world, the church is infected and challenged by racism, the caste system, and tribalism because people do not live the reality of their salvation in their daily life. There is only one thing that will solve that problem, and that is the teaching and revelation of the kingdom of God. When you were naturally born, you became a citizen of your country, which thrives on racial prejudices and cultural pride.

Once you are born again, you become a citizen of God's kingdom. You no longer live based on your natural identity but based on your spiritual birth. Every born-again believer, from every nation and language, is a citizen of the same kingdom. There is no racial preference or discrimination in the kingdom of God. That is why Jesus told us to seek it first.

7. IT IS THE PRIORITY OF JESUS

God's priority is to see His kingdom established on earth, not to see all of us in heaven. Everything Jesus taught and preached focused on that priority. He began His ministry saying, "Repent, for the kingdom of heaven is at hand." There are many people who preach repentance these days, but they do not tell the whole story.

They tell people they need to repent to go to heaven. That is not what Jesus preached.

We need to repent because His kingdom has come. At hand means it is here.

He sent His disciples to heal the sick, raise the dead, cleanse the lepers, and tell them the kingdom of God had come *(Matthew 10:7–8; Luke 10:2–9)*.

There are many people who go around and preach and teach healing, and while some people get healed, they remain hungry and broke. Jesus never preached or taught about healing.

He preached the kingdom and healed the sick. He told us to do the same. He sent His disciples to preach the kingdom of God and to heal the sick. *(Luke 9:2)*

When Nicodemus came to Jesus by night to greet Him, He told him about the kingdom of God *(John 3:3)*. He told another man to follow Him, and when the man asked Him to let him go and bury his father first, He replied,

> **"Let the dead bury their own dead, but you go and preach the kingdom of God." (Luke 9:60)**

Jesus said this was His purpose for coming to the earth.

> **But He said to them, "I must preach the kingdom of God to the other cities also, because for this purpose I have been sent." (Luke 4:43)**

People everywhere are worried about the end times. They want to know when the world is going to end. The disciples of Jesus had the same concern, and they asked Jesus to tell them how to know when the end would come. Jesus gave them (us) a very specific answer to know when the end will come, which we have been ignoring for way too long.

> **And this gospel of the kingdom will be preached in all the world as a witness to all the nations, and then the end will come. (Matthew 24:14)**

After the resurrection, Jesus was with the disciples for forty days. He did not tell them how terrible hell was or about the pain and shame He endured on the cross. He had only one subject to talk to them about—the kingdom of God.

> **To whom He also presented Himself alive after His suffering by many infallible proofs, being seen by them during forty days and speaking of the things pertaining to the kingdom of God. (Acts 1:3)**

If the kingdom of God is the priority of Jesus, it should be our priority as well.

JESUS TOLD US TO PRAY FOR THE KINGDOM TO COME

When Jesus taught us to pray, He told us to pray for His kingdom to come and His will to be done on earth as it is in heaven. Why does the kingdom need to come to earth? Because humans cannot survive without a kingdom.

> **In this manner, therefore, pray: Our Father in heaven, hallowed be Your name. Your kingdom come. Your will be done on earth as it is in heaven. Give us this day our daily bread. And forgive us our debts, as we forgive our debtors. And do not lead us into temptation, but deliver**

us from the evil one. For Yours is the kingdom and the power and the glory forever. Amen. (Matthew 6:9–13)

JESUS CAME TO GIVE US A KINGDOM

Many think that Jesus came to give us a religion and that He started Christianity, and it is a better religion than others. He did not come to start a religion, and He never called any of His followers Christians. He came to give us a kingdom.

> ***Do not fear, little flock, for it is your Father's good pleasure to give you the kingdom. (Luke 12:32)***

> ***And I bestow upon you a kingdom, just as My Father bestowed one upon Me. (Luke 22:29)***

> ***He has delivered us from the power of darkness and conveyed us into the kingdom of the Son of His love. (Colossians 1:13)***

The question is, though Jesus gave us a kingdom, how many of us really know anything about a kingdom or what to do with it?

JESUS TOLD US TO PREACH THE KINGDOM

When Jesus sent out His disciples, He told them specifically what they should preach. They were commanded to preach the kingdom of God.

> ***And as you go, preach, saying, "The kingdom of heaven is at hand." (Matthew 10:7)***

No one in the Old Testament could preach what we preach. The kingdom had not yet arrived. They were looking forward to the coming of the kingdom, and to live in the days that we are living in.

SEEK THE KINGDOM FIRST

Again, Jesus instructed His disciples about the sign of His coming and the end of the age when they asked. Jesus was very specific.

> ***And this gospel of the kingdom will be preached in all the world as a witness to all the nations, and then the end will come. (Matthew 24:14)***

HOW DO WE SEEK GOD'S KINGDOM?

How do we seek His kingdom? If Jesus had said, "I want you all to seek first the United Kingdom," it would have been easy for us. We would book our ticket and fly to the UK. The kingdom of God is an invisible kingdom. It does not come with observation. We seek God's kingdom mainly in prayer. How each person discovers the kingdom varies from person to person. This is an individual thing, just like salvation. Just because I discovered God's kingdom doesn't mean my children will enter it.

When I was growing up, I was taught that seeking the kingdom meant preaching the gospel or getting baptized. Many people that I know entered into ministry without being called to it. They misinterpreted *seeking His kingdom* as being in ministry. That was far from the truth. As a result, I have seen hundreds of believers and pastors living in hunger and lack. I wondered if our God is really a good God. When He opened my eyes to see what He really meant by seeking His kingdom, everything changed in my life.

Some others think that seeking God's kingdom means to get closer to God. How do we get closer to a Person who is already living in us? If you are born again, Christ lives in you, and you are a temple of God.

There is no secret formula that can be applied for everyone. It is individual. When you seek His kingdom with all your heart, you will find it. The message of the kingdom frees you from everything the enemy has imposed on you.

When you seek God's kingdom, the primary thing that will happen is that you will discover your purpose. Why do the majority of people on earth not know why they exist? It is because they are outside of God's kingdom. When you discover your calling, you will find out that your provision is included in your calling. That is why Jesus said:

> **Not everyone who says to Me, "Lord, Lord," shall enter the kingdom of heaven, but he who does the will of My Father in heaven. (Matthew 7:21)**

There are so many religious people on earth today who call Jesus their Lord, but their basic needs are not met. Some of them identify as Christians, Pentecostals, or by the name of various religious denominations.

It is interesting to note that Jesus told us to seek His kingdom first, but He did not tell us how to seek it. There are certain principles that are the same in both the Old and New Testaments. Those principles are applicable when it comes to seeking God's kingdom. Below are some of them.

Prayer: Most importantly, we seek God's kingdom through prayer. This is how it started for Jesus and for the disciples. He taught them how to pray kingdom prayers. Prayer is the incubator in which God's kingdom purposes are conceived and developed in a human spirit. The more time you spend in prayer, the sooner you will become pregnant with God's purpose and calling in your life.

During Jesus' ministry, He spent more time in prayer than interacting with people. Prayer was His main ministry. Prayer is a lost art in many

Christians' lives. Just like our physical body needs oxygen to breathe, our spirit man needs communion with God through prayer.

Prayer is not telling God what to do or just presenting our needs. Prayer is partnering with God to accomplish through us what He wants on the earth. When we partner with Him in what He wants to do, He will provide everything we need. That is why Jesus said that our heavenly Father knows what we need before we ask Him *(Matthew 6:8; 32)*.

The only thing the disciples asked Jesus to teach them was how to pray. After walking with Him for a while, they discovered that the secret behind everything Jesus did was the time He spent in prayer. They wanted to know exactly what He was doing when He woke up early and went to a solitary place by Himself. It is interesting to notice that Jesus did not spend time praying with the disciples. It was a private experience.

For Jesus, spending time with His Father to receive what He was supposed to be manifesting on the earth was called prayer. I don't think Jesus ever spent time with the Father telling Him what to do, telling Him to heal or save anyone, or to give Him His laundry list. In prayer, He was accessing heaven to seek the works His Father had prepared for Him before the foundation of the world.

In prayer, Jesus was receiving a blueprint from heaven of everything He was supposed to do that day. If something was not in the blueprint for that day, then He did not do it. After He finished praying, He went out and manifested the works He saw His Father doing and spoke what He heard His Father speaking *(John 5:19-20; 8:38)*. This is the protocol we need to follow in our lives. This is the purpose of prayer. After you spend time in prayer, if there are no works manifesting, then you haven't really prayed. You might have petitioned or done some religious rituals. Petitioning is what servants do; prayer is for sons and daughters to commune with their Father. Prayer is the key through which you access your Father's throne to know what your Father has prepared for you before the foundation of the world. That is what Jesus was doing when He spent time in prayer.

Jesus told us to ask, seek, and knock. The context of this is to keep asking, keep seeking, and keep knocking. We apply that order when it comes to seeking God's kingdom. We ask Him to reveal it to us. We seek it like a lost treasure. Then we knock wherever we can to know more about it.

When you pray and seek His kingdom, God will put a vision in your heart—we call it a dream, the will of God, passion, or some other title. The Bible says that God's people perish only for two reasons: lack of knowledge and lack of vision (Hosea 4:6; Proverbs 29:18 KJV). A vision is a picture of your future that has not materialized yet. Once you receive a vision from God for your purpose, then over the next five years you need to focus your entire life on learning everything about it and its related subjects. That is the way you prepare.

Some visions or dreams may require you to go to a college or university to earn a degree in certain subjects. If you want to become a medical doctor, lawyer, politician, or work in many other professions, it is imperative that you go to school. No one will become a medical doctor just by revelation alone. If you do, either no one will come to you for treatment, or you will end up in prison! In the kingdom, your vision is very important. If you don't have a vision, you are not in the kingdom—you won't go anywhere with your life, and God cannot provide for you.

Your vision, or dream, or calling is God's way—or system— of providing for you in His kingdom: If you seek God's kingdom, I can guarantee that you will find it. Once you discover God's kingdom, you will find your purpose. That is what God intends for every human being. The reason the majority of the people on this earth do not know their purpose is because they are not in God's kingdom. They are not taught to seek it. I also want to warn you not to make the mistake of trying to make it all happen on your own. If you try to make these things in your life happen, you will surely fail. You need to be led by God. Your life belongs to Him.

When you discover who you are, whose you are, and exactly what you are supposed to be doing— and constantly live in that awareness— then you won't have any need to worry. Jesus's solution for worry is not more fun, watch some movies, and eat some ice cream, but to discover His kingdom and your purpose in it.

There are millions of people who are slaves to a system in which they are not happy or satisfied, and there are millions of people who go hungry every day. The preaching of the kingdom is the solution to both of these problems. That is why Jesus told us to go and preach the gospel of the kingdom. The gospel is not just for taking people to heaven.

The word *gospel* means good news. Good news to a person who is hungry is food. Good news to a poor person is freedom from poverty. Good news to a person who is naked is clothing. Good news to a person who is bound is deliverance. This gospel of the kingdom needs to be applied to every aspect of our life and society. It is the solution for every human problem.

Study the Kingdom: Another way to seek God's kingdom is to study about it. That is why this ministry offer courses online for those who are hungry to learn about their purpose and the kingdom of God. Hundreds of people are being blessed all over the world through these courses.

The Bible tells us to study to shew thyself approved unto God, a workman that needeth not to be ashamed, rightly dividing the word of truth.(2 Timothy 2:15 KJV)

We spend twelve years of our lives for our basic schooling, learning how to survive on the earth that is controlled by the Babylonian system.

Then many go to college for another four or more years to obtain a degree. We do that expecting that we will find a job and make enough money for our survival. What if we spent a fraction of that time studying about God's kingdom and our purpose in it? What would happen to this earth and humanity if every believer in Christ begins to do that?

That is why Jesus spent more than three years with His disciples. He did not lay His hands on them and turn them into mighty apostles. He wanted to walk them through the process of understanding and entering His kingdom.

Many people tell me, "Abraham, I don't see any kingdom and no money appeared on my doorstep to fulfill my purpose either. I have compassion because they do not know what they are talking about, and the sad part is that many will not understand what this book is all about either.

Seek the Kingdom like a treasure hidden in a field: When we are passionate about something, it will show in our words, actions, and in our priorities. The more effort you put into something, the better results we get. The same applies to seeking God's kingdom. Some people practice their favourite sport four to five hours a day. That's how they become a champion. How many hours or days did you spend seeking and studying God's kingdom, the most important subject in the Bible?

SEEK THE KINGDOM FIRST

There's a parable that Jesus shared about the kingdom being like a treasure hidden in a field. A man found it and went and sold all that he had and came back and bought that field. Why did he have to sell everything he had? Why couldn't he keep some of his stuff and add the kingdom of God to what he already had?

We have to prioritize when it comes to God's kingdom. It can't be substituted for anything else or added to something we already know and do. It cannot be compared to any other treasures we have. Nothing is worth keeping if we lose the kingdom. We have to leave all that we were believing and doing prior to discovering His kingdom, just like the disciples did.

To sell all that we have means to leave behind everything we hold as precious on the earth. Sometimes we will have to leave our own parents in order to follow the call of God. All of our religious practices, rituals, and connections must go; we can't take them with us and enter God's kingdom.

This is one of the reasons the kingdom message is not working for many people. When they hear it, they get excited and try to add it to all the other religious things they have already been doing. Or they try to do it now with a new passion. But it doesn't work for them. They will get tired and become burned out pretty soon. If they prayed for ten minutes before now, they try to pray for forty minutes, but that discipline won't last long; it might last for three days. Or they try to go out and witness to people. That is not the kingdom— it's a religious zeal without the knowledge of God.

Follow the calling God has on your life: When God shows us something, it is our responsibility to follow what He showed us. If we just wait for something to happen, nothing will happen. When we make a move in the direction He is leading us, God will move heaven and earth on our behalf. I have a whole book and course on discovering Purpose, Calling, and Gifts. I would highly recommend you take one of these courses. Visit our website: *www.TheKingdomUniversity.org* to sign up for an upcoming course.

After we seek it and discover it, the next step is to enter God's kingdom. To do that, we need to discover God's will for our lives. Sadly, many people these days run after miracles instead. There are many prophetic and healing schools that teach you how to prophesy and pray for the sick, but not very many schools help you discover God's will for your life and teach you how to live in His kingdom.

God's will for my life is not the same as His will for yours. Each of us is equipped to do something different.

> **Therefore, brethren, be even more diligent to make your call and election sure, for if you do these things you will never stumble; for so an entrance will be supplied to you abundantly into the everlasting kingdom of our Lord and Savior Jesus Christ. (2 Peter 1:10–11)**

This verse says that we need to make our calling and election sure. When we do this, we will never stumble. When we are sure of exactly what we are called to do (God's will), an entrance will be supplied to the everlasting kingdom of our Lord and Savior Jesus Christ. Once you seek God's kingdom and discover your purpose, it is still not easy to enter His kingdom. The enemy will fight and do his best to keep you in his fold. As long as you are a good churchgoing Christian, you are not any threat to his kingdom; but the moment you try to renounce the kingdom of this world and enter God's kingdom, all hell will break loose.

We are in the midst of an age-old fight between two kingdoms: the kingdom of God and the kingdom of darkness. They both want human souls.

And when they had preached the gospel to that city and made many disciples, they returned to Lystra, Iconium, and Antioch, strengthening the souls of the disciples, exhorting them to continue in the faith, and saying, "We must through many *tribulations enter the kingdom of God.*" (Acts 14:21-22)

In the process of entering the kingdom, we will go through "many" tribulations. Forces of darkness will fight us to keep us away from the kingdom of our Father. We have a whole book called *Seeing, Entering, and Manifesting the Kingdom* and also a course on that subject at The Kingdom University.

CHAPTER 8

THE MOST LIBERATING MESSAGE

Your kingdom come. Your will be done on earth as it is in heaven. (Matthew 6:10)

WHY IS THE KINGDOM MESSAGE THE MOST LIBERATING MESSAGE IN THE WORLD ?

The kingdom of God has the solution to every problem we will face on earth. It is God's ultimate solution to every human problem. The reason you are having challenges in any area of your life is because you are not sure how that part of your life works in His kingdom. It is like a person traveling in a foreign country and not knowing how the system works in that country.

For example, in the country that I am from, in order to use public transportation to go somewhere, you get on a bus and then you buy the ticket to the place you want to go to from the driver. When I went to New York City, I found that the system there worked differently. You need to buy the ticket in advance, and then get on the bus. You can get into trouble with the authorities if you do not know how things work. It is the same in the spirit.

DISCOVERING THE LOST KINGDOM

We have been born again into a kingdom, but we have not been taught how to benefit from it or how it operates. If you do not know how things work in the kingdom of God, you will have problems. You were born to live in a kingdom.

God saw the earth and how people in it were worried and burdened with the problems of life. He sent His own Son with the solution to all of those problems. The solution is the kingdom of God. The Father told the Son to bring us His kingdom because He saw everyone struggling and dying without it.

BENEFITS OF SEEKING GOD'S KINGDOM

1. IT PROVIDES MAN'S BASIC NEEDS. NO ONE NEEDS TO LIVE IN HUNGER

There is no need for anyone to live in hunger on this planet. You will read more about this later in the book.

2. IT HELPS PEOPLE DISCOVER THEIR PURPOSE

You can't discover God's kingdom and not discover your purpose. It is impossible. Your purpose is connected to His kingdom.

3. IT RESTORES HUMAN VALUE

Jesus said that if our heavenly Father takes care of and provides for the birds of the air and the lilies of the field, He will surely take care of us because we are more valuable than they. You are valuable to God because you are the King's kid.

4. IT LIBERATES MAN FROM POVERTY

Jesus said that He is anointed to preach the gospel to the poor. Why do the poor need the gospel? Because it will bring them back to the kingdom, where they belong. They will discover their purpose and calling, and that will be the end of their poverty.

5. IT IS THE ONLY HOPE FOR HUMANITY

The gospel of the kingdom is the only message that God gave us to preach. Every other message we preach is a subsidiary of the kingdom message, or an aspect of it. The kingdom is the only hope for humanity.

6. IT LIBERATES MAN FROM A CASTE SYSTEM AND RACISM

As I mentioned, the only message that will unify the people of the world is the message of the kingdom. People are divided based on their country, their race, their color, and their language. Although we have been preaching Jesus, even the body of Christ is divided and scattered. Knowing that we all belong to the same kingdom (same country) and serve the same King should bring down the walls that divide and separate us.

7. IT ALLOWS US TO LIVE FREE FROM WORRY

Knowing the kingdom of God is what we need, our Lord Jesus Christ specifically commanded us not to worry. In Matthew 6:25–34, Jesus taught His disciples the secret to worry-free living. They were working men, and they had businesses to support their families. When Jesus called them, they left their businesses and followed Him. They did not sell their businesses and collect the savings to support their families for a while. It was a sudden change from having income to support them to having no income the next day.

In today's world, especially in the West, we can't leave what we have to follow Jesus and His calling. We are so tied to the Babylonian system that almost everything we use is owned or financed by banks. If we don't make payments on time, we may end up in jail or lose everything. The enemy has set up his system so well that it is almost impossible for people to follow what God has called them to do. It scares them to step out.

A fisherman's income depended on what they caught each day. If something like that happened in our society, it would be shocking. What if the main breadwinner loses his or her job without any warning? Or what if something tragic happens to someone in the family? How does life go on after that?

Of course, life does go on. That is what Jesus was teaching them—how to live without depending on the world system and how to live in His kingdom. His disciples were worried about where the next meal was going to come from and how they were going to support their families. In response to their apprehension,

He said,

> *Therefore I say to you, do not worry about your life, what you will eat or what you will drink; nor about your body, what you will put on. Is not life more than food and the body more than clothing? Look at the birds of the air, for they neither sow nor reap nor gather into barns; yet your heavenly Father feeds them. Are you not of more value than they? Which of you by worrying can add one cubit to his stature?*
>
> *So why do you worry about clothing? Consider the lilies of the field, how they grow: they neither toil nor spin; and yet I say to you that even Solomon in all his glory was not arrayed like one of these. Now if God so clothes*

> *the grass of the field, which today is, and tomorrow is thrown into the oven, will He not much more clothe you, O you of little faith?*
>
> *Therefore do not worry, saying, "What shall we eat?" or "What shall we drink?" or "What shall we wear?" For after all these things the Gentiles seek.*
>
> *For your heavenly Father knows that you need all these things. But seek first the kingdom of God and His righteousness, and all these things shall be added to you. Therefore do not worry about tomorrow, for tomorrow will worry about its own things. Sufficient for the day is its own trouble. (Matthew 6:25–34, emphasis added)*

Jesus said three times in that one passage not to worry. That means it is very important to Him. When we worry, we are not displaying a good witness to the rest of creation that He is a good Father. It leaves a bad impression about His character, and He takes that very personally.

God never intended for you to worry about anything. Worry is a virus from the enemy's kingdom that causes your mind and body to malfunction. Worry-free living is not a mental ascent or euphoric feeling you achieve by repeating some religious mantra. The culture of His kingdom is righteousness, peace, and joy in the Holy Spirit. Worry is not part of God's nature or His kingdom.

It is the knowledge of the truth about the situation you are worried about that sets you free from worrying. God says in His Word, "My people are destroyed for lack of knowledge" (Hosea 4:6; Isaiah 5:13).

The lies of the enemy, combined with doubt, bring worry. We tend to worry about things that are out of our control. You are worried about an area of your life because you believe a lie of the enemy and lack the revelation of God about it.

Maybe you heard what God said about worrying, but it has not yet become revelation in your spirit. Just because you know something does not mean you are benefiting from it. When the knowledge you have grows into understanding, it becomes revelation. Revelation is the key to your breakthrough.

If you worry about money, it means you do not know what God says about your finances in His kingdom. To be free from worrying about money, you need an understanding of how God's economic system works. I call it Kingdom Economy.

If you are worried about your health or are sick in your body, you are not sure of how the healthcare system works in His kingdom; and, most likely, what God says about what you should and should not eat. I call it Kingdom Agriculture.

If you are worried about being able to meet the basic needs of your family, you do not understand the foundational principles of His kingdom and how our King relates to His children.

If you are worried about relationships or family, you are not functioning according to biblical principles for relationship and family. I call it Kingdom Family.

You worry when you are doing something you are not created to do. You worry because of a lack of trust in God. You worry because you want to be in control. When we worry, we question God's faithfulness. Will He provide? Will He protect? Will He do what He said He would do? When you are sure of your provision, purpose, and protection, you will stop worrying.

THE MOST LIBERATING MESSAGE

There are three major areas of worry. First, the majority of people in the world are worried about meeting their basic needs (food, shelter, and clothing). According to UN statistics, at least eighty percent of humanity lives on less than ten dollars a day. Twenty percent live on less than a dollar a day. The second reason people worry is because they are trying to control a future event that is not here yet. The third reason is regret, wishing they could go back and fix something in the past.

Controlling the future and fixing the past are both impossible. Worry is one of the most futile things you can do; it has no benefit whatsoever, but plenty of side effects. It is also one of the most harmful things you can do to yourself, like smoking or drinking.

Worrying about something won't change anything. To change something, you need to gain new knowledge and take action based on that knowledge. I wish I could regain all the time that I spent worrying in the past. I could have written ten more books! Worrying creates anxiety, which leads to stress, and eventually, depression and all sorts of physical problems.

You can be a good Christian and still be broke. You can be a Spirit-filled believer and still not know your purpose. You can be a tongue-talking Jesus follower and be sick in your body. You can be called to ministry and still starve. But when you discover God's kingdom, you cannot live broke, sick, hungry, or full of worry anymore. In His kingdom, you will find everything you need—healing, provision, peace, purpose, etc.

Jesus used two of His creations to teach us a lesson about worrying. Everything God created reveals an aspect of His glory. He has hidden the laws that govern life and the mysteries of His kingdom in the things He created. That is why when Jesus taught in His parables about the mysteries of His kingdom, He used things He created. In this lesson, He used the birds of the air and lilies of the field to teach us the secret behind not worrying.

Jesus's solution for people who were worried about what they were going to eat, drink, and wear was to seek the kingdom of God. That means before we do anything in life, the first thing we need to do is seek His kingdom. He did not say to seek a good church, good education, or a better job. No. He knew that man was worrying about all these things because we'd lost God's kingdom. Those basic necessities are part of His kingdom. I believe that if Jesus were to come today, He would preach the same message He preached two thousand years ago. He wouldn't tell you to go to a famous university and get a good education first, so that you will be able to find a good job and make a living. No, He would not.

Is Jesus against getting a good education? He is not. I'm not against it, either. What He's saying is that education is not the requirement in His kingdom, and that is not how it operates. A person doesn't enter His kingdom based on his or her educational qualifications; His kingdom is made of laws and principles that will work for anyone, at any time, in any place. There is definitely a place for education in His kingdom, but that is not the source of our income, provision, identity, value, or significance

It's possible to be a Christian and not live in the Father's kingdom or know much about it. I was a Christian who lived in lack and scarcity. I went to church four times a week and was forced to fast twice a week. In spite of all that, I didn't know anything about God's kingdom.

Jesus told us to look at the birds of the air. He did not say to look at the birds that are in a zoo or in a cage at a pet store. Why the birds of the air? What does He want us to learn from the birds? Every

THE MOST LIBERATING MESSAGE

day they wake up singing. I hear their singing at four o'clock in the morning. Have you ever seen a bird storing up food for the next day? They know that tomorrow will take care of itself. Their provision is part of the system God established. If God created something, He is responsible for taking care of it.

Birds are created to be in the air. Why is air important to birds? Birds don't eat air. Birds need food to eat and air to fly because they are created for it. A bird will never worry about flying. That is their domain. When they are at the place of their function and purpose, they are not worried about anything. Everything God created has a place and purpose. He said, "Your heavenly Father feeds them. Are you not of more value than they?" (Matthew 6:26).

Can you imagine God feeding the innumerable number of creatures He created—those in the air, in the forest, and in the water—every single day? I have never seen a bird working overtime trying to feed itself and its family. I have been to some of the poorest areas on this earth, and I still haven't seen a bird hesitant to go home in the evening because it didn't get enough food. But I have seen and read almost daily about thousands of human beings starving and dying of hunger.

Statistics say that more than twenty thousand people die every day of hunger or hunger-related causes. My question is why? Doesn't God care about these people more than He cares for the birds?

When the Israelites came out of Egypt, who fed them? The Bible says there were six hundred thousand men and their wives and children! That was probably close to three million people, plus their livestock. God fed them all for forty years! He provided manna, meat, and water for them. Imagine how many truckloads of food and water were needed to feed three million people a day! An average family of four needs forty thousand US dollars a year to survive. How much would it cost for six hundred thousand families a year?

The second part of creation Jesus used to teach us not to worry is the lilies of the field. Again, He specified lilies of the field. Lilies are created to be in the field. They don't eat the field, but it is necessary for their survival. They are not trying to grow and become something. They grow and bring forth their flowers. Have you seen a tree trying to grow, or a lily working hard to produce its flowers? It all happens as part of a natural process.

Why do so many people in this world struggle to meet their basic needs? Many think their number one problem is a lack of food and clothing. They think that if they have food and clothing, they have a life. According to Jesus, that is not true. He said, "Is not life more than food and the body more than clothing?" (Matthew 6:25). That means your life needs something more important than food and your body is made for something more important than clothing. What could that be? Your life is not meant to be spent working for food or things that perish with use. Jesus said,

> ***"Do not labor for the food which perishes, but for the food which endures to everlasting life, which the Son of Man will give you, because God the Father has set His seal on Him." (John 6:27)***

We have been taught that food and clothing are the number one things we need for survival. But Jesus said that He will provide those if we seek something different.

People who are alive and have food to eat are not necessarily fulfilling their purpose or living a life of fulfillment. What is the purpose of our body? Our body is made to be the temple of God.

THE MOST LIBERATING MESSAGE

This means that our body gives God and our spirit the legal right to operate on the earth. To live and operate on earth requires a physical body. That is why evil spirits look for a body to enter. We have made our body all about eating food and wearing clothing. How sad!

The only creatures that are not happy to be what God created them to be are humans. A bird is happy to be a bird. A tree is happy to be a tree. But if you look at man, he is not happy to be a man. He is trying to be something else. In our society today, there is much confusion about gender and identity. Men are trying to be women, and women are trying to be men. Imagine a man confused about which bathroom he should use! Sadly, confusion and chaos have become constants in our society. Women are not happy with the way God created them, so they spend billions of dollars on artificial beauty.

Birds are doing what they were born to do. God feeds them, but that does not mean He brings their food to their nests. No, they still have to go and find it. That is their purpose. The lilies are doing what they are created to do. Birds wake up early in the morning, singing about the day, while we are hesitant to wake up at all. Why do many people hate to go to do their job on Monday? Because they know that what they are doing is not what they were born to do.

As I mentioned, everything God created has a purpose and a place to fulfill it. Birds need air to fly, fish need water to swim in, and plants need the field to grow. If you remove a bird from the air, it will not live as God intended. If you remove a fish from the water, it will die. And if you remove a plant from the field, it too will wither and die.

Is it possible that the reason thousands of humans die every day from hunger and remain hopeless is because they are not in the right place fulfilling their purpose? That is what Jesus said. When He looked at the crowd, He saw that they were all worried about what they were going to eat, drink, and wear. He saw them living like orphans—without a Father or a purpose and struggling to survive.

You might say that humans are created to live on the earth. Yes, that is true, so are all other creatures. Then why do these and many more die and remain hopeless? Man needs something more than just earth to live on. If the air and field are not food for the birds and the lilies, then what is man's air and field? What I mean is, according to God's perspective, what is required other than food for man to live?

Birds can live in a house or in a cage, but that is not the place of their optimal function. They are created to be free in the air. Each creation requires an environment for its optimal function. Fish can live in an aquarium, but that is not the place they were created to be. Even different fish require different types, or bodies, of water. Man can live on the earth, but he needs a specific environment for his optimal function and purpose. All plants and creatures do not grow just anywhere; they all require a particular atmosphere.

When God created Adam, he didn't just put him anywhere on earth. The Lord created a very specific environment for him to live in and function. He knew that for this man to function at his full potential, he required something more than just earth. So the Lord planted a garden called Eden (kingdom of God). The Bible says God took him and put him in the garden. He did not take him to the bush or to the jungle but to a garden. Why?

Every product of value comes with a manual. If you read the manual, the manufacturer clearly mentions the environment that the product needs for it to work effectively. It will tell you about the temperature and different conditions the product requires, as well as the environments to stay away from for it to operate as the manufacturer intended. If those conditions are not met, the product will malfunction.

THE MOST LIBERATING MESSAGE

Man was created to live in a garden-like environment. When I say garden, I don't necessarily mean a place with flowers and plants. The first thing that comes to my mind when I think of a garden is order and beauty. The Bible says our God is a God of order. He has made everything beautiful. Another thing that comes to my mind is productivity or fruitfulness. The first commandment God gave to man was to be fruitful (Genesis 1:28). If something is not fruitful in a garden, it gets cut down and replaced with something else. A garden needs to be protected, cultivated, and nurtured.

A garden also represents nature. In nature, God hid everything mankind needs to know concerning Himself and His kingdom. Jesus used things from nature in most of His parables to reveal the mysteries of His kingdom.

> *For since the creation of the world His invisible attributes are clearly seen, being understood by the things that are made, even His eternal power and Godhead, so that they are without excuse. (Romans 1:20)*

> *Then the LORD God took the man and put him in the garden of Eden to tend and keep it. And the LORD God commanded the man, saying, "Of every tree of the garden you may freely eat." (Genesis 2:15–16)*

> *He who did not spare His own Son, but delivered Him up for us all, how shall He not with Him also freely give us all things? (Romans 8:32)*

Adam's food, shelter, and clothing were already prepared for him. That's the way God's kingdom operates. God will never send you to a place where He hasn't prepared provision for you. He told Elijah to go to Zarephath where He had commanded a widow to provide for him (1 Kings 17:9).

DISCOVERING THE LOST KINGDOM

Our God is a King. We are kings with a little "k." Kings require a place of dominion. Every man has the desire to build, cultivate, manage, establish, and rule. If he cannot do those things, he gets frustrated. We are designed and created to live in a kingdom. Without a kingdom, man cannot exist—good or evil. Man was created to be a king on the earth and have dominion.

Adam's calling was to tend and keep the garden. His food and all other needs were included in His calling— even his wife. God brought her to the garden, the place of his purpose. He didn't have to do a separate job to feed himself and his family. Many people are not finding their mate these days because they are not at the place of their calling.

When Adam disobeyed God, he lost the garden—the environment required for his function and purpose. He began to feel hunger, hopelessness, and worry outside of the garden. As long as Adam was in the garden, he did not lack anything. As long as you are in God's kingdom, you won't lack anything, either.

Ever since then, man has been trying to create a substitute for what he lost using the things of the earth, but it never even comes close. The enemy of man began to offer him luxury, comfort, fun, the pleasures of this world, and all sorts of things as a substitute for what he lost. But it never satisfies his soul; instead, it hurts people more and destroys them in the end.

Adam did not fall from heaven. When he fell, he did not lose heaven. He lost a kingdom because his relationship with God was broken. When God decided to save or reconcile man to Himself, He sent His Son with a special gift. He did not come with a bunch of philosophies or theories like other religious leaders. He did not come with a revival message.

THE MOST LIBERATING MESSAGE

He brought to man what we lost in the garden. He brought the kingdom of God to us.

If God had sent His Son to save fish that were dying without water, He would have sent Him with water. If God was trying to save birds that were dying without air, He would have come with air. He would not come with a philosophy or a religion. That is not what they needed.

Jesus came with one message that He preached day in and day out. This was the message of the kingdom of God, knowing that it was what people needed the most—people who were full of anxiety over what they were going to eat, drink, and wear. Seek God's kingdom, and you will find everything you need.

HOW DOES SEEKING GOD'S KINGDOM MEET MAN'S BASIC NEEDS?

As we saw, instead of taking us all back into a garden, God put His kingdom within us. He promised to take care and provide for anyone interested in fulfilling His assignment. Now it's up to us to bring His rule and domain wherever we go and through whatever we do. That is the purpose of our existence. We are His garden, and He is the Gardener.

People thought their main problem was a lack of food, water, and clothing. But in God's sight, that was not their primary problem. Humans were created to live in God's kingdom. Without it, they will not survive long, no matter how much money or talent they may have. Just think of some famous and rich people you have heard of who took their own lives or died prematurely.

Every human being on this earth is hungering for one thing: the kingdom of God. But not everyone realizes it because not everyone knows the whole story. Until they discover and find their place in it, they will never be fully satisfied.

DISCOVERING THE LOST KINGDOM

In Matthew 6, Jesus said people were hungry, naked, and worried about their life, but not because of a lack of education or employment. They were not in the place God created them to be, so He told them to seek the kingdom of God first.

You can be a Christian for many years and still be longing for something. If you are, that means you are not living in God's kingdom yet. Some look for the rapture, and many others look for another revival. When you find God's kingdom, you will not long for anything else; you will not long for a revival. Your soul will find its home and you will find rest.

That is why Jesus said, "Come to Me, all you who labor and are heavy laden, and I will give you rest." (Matthew 11:28)

Rest does not mean you will not do any more work, but you will be doing a different kind of work: the work your heavenly Father sent you to do (Ephesians 2:10). Today, most people don't have any time to do what God created them to do because they are busy trying to provide for themselves.

That is why they hate to go to their job on Monday morning and can't wait for Friday or the next vacation. The majority of the people who are alive on the earth today will live their whole lives and die without ever knowing or fulfilling their calling.

Why do the poor need to hear the gospel of the kingdom? The poor need food, shelter, and clothing. That is what Jesus said He will provide when we seek His kingdom.

> **The blind see and the lame walk; the lepers are cleansed and the deaf hear; the dead are raised up and the poor have the gospel preached to them. (Matthew 11:5)**

THE MOST LIBERATING MESSAGE

Why do the rich need to hear the gospel of the kingdom? Money won't buy eternal life or an entry into the kingdom of God. It doesn't matter how much wealth we have; it will not satisfy us until we discover God's kingdom.

> ***And He said to them, "Take heed and beware of covetousness, for one's life does not consist in the abundance of the things he possesses." (Luke 12:15)***

We have been preaching the gospel of salvation and people have been waiting to go to heaven, but they are in debt, hungry, and broke because they have no revelation of the kingdom of God. I spent five years in Bible school and did a lot of other short-term training in missions with different organizations, but I never had a course on the kingdom of God—the most important message Jesus preached and commanded us to preach.

GOD PROVIDING FOR OUR NEEDS

Why does God want to meet our basic needs? Why is it His responsibility? When a child is born, it is the responsibility of the parents to provide for and protect that child. Food, clothing, shelter, and everything else that child needs will be provided according to the capacity of the parents. They provide until that child is grown and mature and able to support himself. It is the same in God's kingdom.

In His kingdom, He will provide for your basic needs until you discover your calling. Then, fulfilling your calling adds the things you need and want in your life. When you are born again, you become a child of God. The first thing you should be seeking after that should be His kingdom, not some religious experience.

He wants to meet our basic needs so we can spend our time doing what He created us to do here. That is why the kingdom message is the most liberating message in this universe. It is not the responsibility of the government of your country to provide for your food. Jesus said our heavenly Father knows that we need all of these things. He knows we need these things, whether we ask for them or not. We don't feed our children because they ask for food. We do it because we know they need it, before they ask.

Most people spend the majority of their time working a job to provide for their family. In the kingdom of God, He provides our basic needs so you and I can focus on our calling. Many people spend excessive hours at their workplace, trying to support their family, just to end up losing their family because they are never home. That is not God's will.

When you are forced to do what you don't like to do, but you have to do it for your survival, it is abuse or slavery. Jesus came to set the captives free. The world's system—or our culture— says money is our biggest problem or need. To make money, you need to go to school and get an education. Why? When you have an education, you can find a job that helps you make money so you can pay your bills and buy food.

If you ask most people why they work, their reply would be, "to pay bills," or "to buy food," or something similar. Jesus said that if you seek His kingdom first, He will provide your basic needs and help you focus on discovering your purpose and calling. Once you find your specific calling, your provision is included in it.

The devil does not want you to know this; neither does he want you to discover your purpose. He wants to keep you religious and busy, looking forward to some spiritual experience that is going to happen someday or in the sweet by-and-by. As long as you are looking forward to experiencing what God has promised in the future, you will never experience it now. Faith says, "Now!"

THE MOST LIBERATING MESSAGE

Next, we are going to see the fundamental needs of all human beings and how God designed meeting all of them through His kingdom.

CHAPTER 9

EIGHT FUNDAMENTAL NEEDS OF EVERY HUMAN

And my God shall supply all your need according to His riches in glory by Christ Jesus. (Philippians 4:19)

Humans have three basic physical needs: food, clothing, and shelter. We are not just a body. God created man as a three-part being, consisting of spirit, soul, and body, and each of those components has specific needs. If they are not all met, one will feel as if something is out of place in his or her life. God cares about each of these components and every need.

It is God's design that all of our needs are met through Him and His kingdom. When Adam fell, he lost the garden of Eden, which was the kingdom of God. Ever since, mankind has been trying to meet our needs outside of God's kingdom.

Humans have eight fundamental needs; and when they are met, our physical, emotional, and spiritual needs are all covered. When one of those needs is not met, we will feel unfulfilled or like something is missing. When God created Adam, He knew man needed other things besides a relationship with his Creator to function on earth. Believe it or not, your relationship with God, or Jesus, is not enough.

Don't be shocked because I said Jesus is not enough. This isn't just my opinion. Jesus Himself told us to seek His kingdom first, not Him. There is a very specific reason for this. God created mankind in such a way that we have other needs aside from having a relationship with Him. But through our relationship with Him, we will find the way to meet those needs legitimately. If you don't believe me, just look in the mirror or at the believers around you. People everywhere are working hard to meet these eight needs.

We are going to see how God set it up so that all of these needs are met through His kingdom.

1. RELATIONSHIP WITH GOD

If God is love (which He is), why is it so difficult for many people to relate to Him and understand Him? Why do most people have a hard time receiving His love, including believers? The first time we see God connecting with Adam is in the garden of Eden, which was His kingdom. Do you want to meet God? Visit Him *in His kingdom*.

We find God's love in His kingdom because love is the culture of the kingdom. We are family, His sons and daughters in the kingdom. Outside of His kingdom, we are nothing.

Any relationship we seek with God outside of His kingdom is in the context of religion. God never intended to relate with mankind outside of His kingdom. After the fall of Adam, God had to use other methods like promises, covenants, and laws to relate with mankind.

God refuses to relate, protect, and provide for mankind outside of His kingdom. Even if He talks with a heathen, it will be in the context of His kingdom. That's why God doesn't protect and provide for everyone who is in need. However, He will overthrow kings and kingdoms and go to any extent to protect one of His citizens in His kingdom.

Once we are in the kingdom, we will no longer be dependent on promises or covenants. We will be able to connect with Him as Father and children once again, like Adam did before the fall.

Even in the New Testament, God did not intend to connect with humans apart from His kingdom. That is why Jesus came preaching the kingdom and the arrival of His kingdom. He didn't come preaching about the love of God; that wasn't His primary message. His main message was the kingdom. The kingdom is very important to Jesus and His Father, and it is critical to our relationship with Him.

It's very possible to think you are living for God but serve the devil and his kingdom instead. The Jewish people in Jesus's day thought they were serving God and were holy. In truth, they were being deceived and used by the devil to accomplish his will *(John 8:44)*. That is the deception of religion.

2. A COUNTRY OR COMMUNITY

Your heart and spirit have been longing for a country or a community. Until we find the place our heart is longing for, we won't feel settled or at home in our spirit. Every purpose requires a particular atmosphere for fulfillment, just as each seed requires an environment that suits its growth. That is why the Bible says that when God created Adam, He did not just leave him stranded on earth. He created a garden for him to dwell in and fulfill His purpose. God took Adam and put him in the garden of Eden.

Jesus told us to seek a place or His country first before seeking anything else *(Matthew 6:33)*.

3. A GOVERNMENT THAT ADMINISTERS RIGHTEOUSNESS, JUSTICE, TRUTH, AND MERCY

Every few years, we elect new people to positions of authority, expecting they will get it right and administer justice and truth. But politicians and governments keep failing us, though we keep trying year after year. Only the kingdom of God can provide the stability and safety we are looking for— no other form of government can do that. No earthly government will work without God being the center of it. Government originated in Him; it's His idea. That's why everyone talks about government. Even a remote village in the Sahara has a leader or a village head. That is government. We can't function without a government.

4. SIGNIFICANCE

Your purpose in life is what makes you feel significant, and it is where you find acceptance and appreciation from others. Why do people do crazy things like painting their hair blue or green? Why do they deform their faces with holes, metal, and screws? They do it to feel significant and attract the attention of others. Only discovering and fulfilling our purpose can give us true significance.

5. FOOD AND SHELTER

The reason you go to work in the morning is to make money to pay for your food and shelter. The majority of our time on earth is spent trying to make a living. People everywhere are concerned about what they will eat and where they will live. Jesus told us not to worry about what we will eat or wear but to seek His kingdom first, and all those things would be added to us.

EIGHT FUNDAMENTAL NEEDS OF EVERY HUMAN

6. FULFILLING RELATIONSHIPS

We were created for relationship. Without relationships, we will not survive or fulfill our purpose. We can't do what God has called us to do alone. Because people's relationship with God is not properly aligned, they encounter problems with others. Every other relationship we have is a reflection of our relationship with God. Not long after God created Adam, He said that it wasn't good for him to be alone *(Genesis 2:18)*.

Of everything He created in Genesis, that was the only thing He said was not good.

Marriage is a kingdom concept, and since God conducted the first marriage in the kingdom (in the garden) for the purpose of accomplishing His kingdom assignment, marriage won't work outside of God's kingdom and outside of the purpose for which it was designed. It doesn't matter how much money we spend or what status we hold in the community; marriage outside of God's kingdom is hard work and vanity.

When a man and a woman are fully united in their spirit, soul, and body, and completely aligned with God and His kingdom to fulfill His assignment on earth, marriage becomes heaven on earth. This was God's original idea for marriage. Instead, when it becomes focused on money, sex, beauty, jewelry, gifts, social status, toys, egos, and self, it becomes stressful, emotionally draining, and hell on earth instead of a blessing.

7. SAFETY

Everyone wants to feel safe. The safest place on earth is in the kingdom of God, in the center of His will. You could be thrown into a furnace or a lion's den, and you would be safe.

8. HAPPINESS

Adam met with God every day and they walked and talked. That was the source of man's joy. The Bible says there is fullness of joy and pleasures in His presence *(Psalm 16:11)*. When you lose the joy that comes from knowing God, you will need the things of this world to make you happy or to have fun.

The entertainment and sports industries have been trying to keep us happy with their productions. It's not rare to read in the news that people who are part of those industries die at a very young age. They entertain others by sacrificing themselves, without knowing whom they are serving with their life. By the time they realize the truth, it is often too late to turn around.

EIGHT FUNDAMENTAL NEEDS OF EVERY HUMAN

GOD

Place: A country or community where they are happy

Power: Government of Righteousness, Justice, Truth, Mercy

Purpose: Significance

Provision: Food and shelter

Person: Fulfilling relationships

Protection: Safety

Pleasure: Happiness

THE SEVEN P'S

Everything we do in life is geared toward meeting one of the needs mentioned above. And God has orchestrated in His divine wisdom that once you discover His kingdom, He will meet all of those needs. Through Jesus, we are supposed to discover His kingdom, just as Adam found Eden through God. Only when we discover His kingdom will all of these needs be met legitimately. From a kingdom perspective, we are all looking for seven P's.

1. PLACE

The first is a place. That place is the kingdom. People in developing nations interpret this as migrating to a developed country. People in developed countries think it is moving to a better part of town or a bigger house. However, once we move, we realize that places and things quickly lose significance.

2. POWER

Humans love power, but most of the time we misuse it. We are looking for power to control our circumstances and the events happening around us. There are different kinds of power: money, influence, political, military, spiritual, and demonic power.

The kingdom of God is the source of all true power and authority. When you rediscover your purpose and live out your calling using the gifts God has given you, it will automatically bring you power. All authority flows from Him.

3. PURPOSE

Without purpose, life is meaningless. Whatever we do, if we are not fulfilling our purpose, we will feel unfulfilled. Every person is looking for his or her purpose. When you discover the kingdom of God, you will discover your purpose. Purpose will bring significance.

EIGHT FUNDAMENTAL NEEDS OF EVERY HUMAN

4. PROVISION

Our physical body requires food, and God is aware of that need. When He created Adam, He also planted a garden in the east and put him in it to tend and keep it. Adam's food was included in that garden.

5. PERSON

We are created to have an intimate relationship with at least one other person. When we don't have that, we will feel unfulfilled. We are created for companionship and connection. It begins with our relationship with our parents, then friends, then a life partner, coworkers, and so on. In the kingdom, the most important relationship is the one we have with the King. Every other relationship we have is a reflection of our relationship with Him.

6. PROTECTION

We all want to feel safe and protected. The kingdom of God is the safest place to be because there is no one greater or stronger than our King Jesus.

7. PLEASURE

Since we lost the kingdom, people everywhere are looking for some form of entertainment to be happy. It is a desire of every human heart. Righteousness, peace, and joy in the Holy Spirit compose the culture of the kingdom of God.

THE KINGDOM MEETS THE NEEDS

Throughout history, people in every culture have been looking to meet these eight needs. No system, religion, or government has been able to meet these needs for us yet. People everywhere are disappointed and feeling unfulfilled. Man has not ended his search yet. People are born with an instinct or hunger that says there is a place and a person somewhere out there; if they can discover it, all their needs will be met.

It doesn't matter how great or anointed you are or how close you are to God; none of that will be a substitute for these needs. Before the fall, Adam was the most anointed person—other than Jesus Christ—who ever walked on earth. He was one with God and covered with His glory.

The reason great and anointed men and women make mistakes or fall is because they try to meet their needs outside of God's kingdom. The enemy recognizes an unmet need in their life and presents them with an opportunity to meet it through a temptation. They fall prey to it, and it destroys them and others.

People everywhere keep trying new methods but come across the same fate as others before them. They are left wounded and broken. Is there a solution to this dilemma? Is there a system, person, or place where they will be able to have all of their needs met? I believe there is.

I believe that man's search for this place and person that fulfills all their needs will end only when they rediscover the kingdom of God and Jesus Christ, their King. We have been telling people that God, or Jesus, will fill the void in their lives, but I have seen people with Jesus in their lives still feeling empty and unfulfilled.

We forget to tell them that Jesus is the way or the door to a place. He is the way to our heavenly Father and the door to His kingdom. We separated Him from His kingdom, and offered just Jesus to the people. They only received part of the gospel; though they received Him, they are still walking around empty with unmet needs.

EIGHT FUNDAMENTAL NEEDS OF EVERY HUMAN

Once they come to Jesus *and* discover His kingdom, they will find the keys to fulfilling relationships, and they will discover their purpose. That will give them significance and everything else they need. The kingdom of God is a country whose culture is made of righteousness, peace, and joy. That is real peace and pleasure.

The kingdom of God has a government that administers righteousness, justice, truth, and mercy. When you're in the kingdom of God, you will know that it is the safest place to be and that it has an unlimited supply of resources, both natural and spiritual. This is where you will feel the most secure and protected, regardless of where you are on the earth. As I mentioned earlier, you could be thrown into a lion's den and still be safe. God and His kingdom are everlasting and unshakable *(Psalm 145:13; Hebrews 12:28)*.

That is why Jesus said, "Seek *first* the kingdom of God and His righteousness, and all these things shall be added to you" *(Matthew 6:33, emphasis added)*. When you discover God's kingdom, your search for the *place* will end. You can't discover His kingdom without meeting the King. When you meet Jesus, the King, your search for a *person* will end.

When you discover the kingdom, you will finally understand your *purpose*. When you fulfill your purpose, you will feel significant. You will understand the true *power* God has made available for you in His kingdom *(Romans 8:11; Ephesians 1:19)*. When you live in His kingdom, you will feel His *protection* around you 24/7.

Nothing gives you more pleasure than knowing God and doing His will. Once you understand true joy, you will find out that all other pleasures and fun were just counterfeits. How does God plan to meet our needs? When Jesus taught the Kingdom Prayer (which many people refer to as the Lord's Prayer), He included these eight fundamental needs in that prayer. Prayer is how we connect with God. That's why He included the kingdom in the prayer. That is what we are going to find out about next.

CHAPTER 10

THE KINGDOM PRAYER: KEYS TO MEETING ALL OUR NEEDS

And I will give you the keys of the kingdom of heaven, and whatever you bind on earth will be bound in heaven, and whatever you loose on earth will be loosed in heaven. (Matthew 16:19)

Jesus never taught His disciples how to heal the sick, how to cast out a demon, or how to prophesy in a classroom setting. Instead, He demonstrated these things in practical lessons. One thing He taught them was how to pray. Most born-again believers do not pray the Lord's Prayer. They think it is a religious prayer. It is not a religious prayer; it is a kingdom prayer. Everything related to our lives is included in the Lord's Prayer. It covers the spiritual, physical, and social aspects of our lives. I did not understand this for a long time.

Why didn't Jesus teach us how to pray to heal the sick or various types of sicknesses? Why didn't He teach us to pray for prosperity or how to cast out different kinds of demons? Jesus taught us to pray only one kind of prayer. In that single prayer, He included everything we need in our life.

DISCOVERING THE LOST KINGDOM

Do you remember the eight fundamental needs of every human mentioned in the last chapter? The kingdom prayer (the Lord's Prayer) is laid out in a way that addresses each of those needs. This prayer is the key to meeting all of those needs and to living in His kingdom.

It was God who came up with those eight fundamental needs. The first man had those needs and God met each of them through His kingdom. Since Adam lost the kingdom with the fall, those needs have rarely been met. Ever since, mankind has been trying to meet those needs outside or without God and His kingdom. As a result, we created a mess.

With the coming of Jesus, God our Father restored His kingdom back to us. With the restoration of His kingdom, we are once again privileged to have all of those needs met through His kingdom.

With the help of the Holy Spirit, I am going to show you how God has included those eight needs in that single prayer. We gave that prayer to the Catholic Church; and every time they meet, they recite it.

As a result, they became the most powerful church politically, financially, and organizationally, though they veered off doctrinally.

What happened to the church is this: we got the doctrines right (at least we think), but became messed up in how we function, or operate. We became fragmented into millions of pieces and lost our effectiveness. If we get all the doctrines right, we won't be fragmented into pieces. Catholic churches function and operate well as an organization. If they receive the right doctrines, and if we receive the right way to function, then we will win this entire earth for Jesus, our King, in no time. That is God's will and plan.

Below, you will see that those eight fundamental needs align perfectly with the kingdom prayer.

THE KINGDOM PRAYER: KEYS TO MEETING ALL OUR NEEDS

1. RELATIONSHIP WITH GOD

Our Father in heaven, hallowed be Your name.

The first and foremost need of a human being is his or her relationship with God. Father means source. Since He is our Source, there is no real life, meaning, or truth to life apart from Him. The first time and place God interacted with mankind was in the garden of Eden, which was His kingdom. God never intended to relate with mankind outside of His kingdom.

The reason Christianity and the church became a religion and a religious institution is because we began to seek and connect with God outside of His kingdom context. We neglected His kingdom and went after the glitter of the world.

God hesitates to connect with mankind outside of His kingdom. If He does, it is to bring someone back into His kingdom. That is what we see in the Lord's Prayer. God wanted to connect with humans only on the basis of His kingdom and within the parameters of His kingdom assignment; that was His original plan. That is why Jesus came preaching the kingdom. He had no plan of meeting with mankind outside of His kingdom.

Prayer is how we connect with God. When He taught on prayer, Jesus included His kingdom as part of the prayer. This means that the prayers He will answer are those prayers in relation to His kingdom. That might be one of the reasons many of our prayers go unanswered; they have nothing to do with His kingdom (James 4:3).

That is why Jesus said any prayers we pray according to His will, He will answer. What is His will? His will is for His kingdom to come and for His will to be done on earth as it is in heaven. He will answer that (1 John 5:14). He is committed to His will.

Every other will God has revealed in the Bible is subsidiary to His main will, which is for His kingdom to come and for His will to be done on earth as it is in heaven. For example, it is God's will that we are saved. The reason He wants us to be saved is because He wants us in His kingdom doing His assignment.

2. A COUNTRY OR COMMUNITY WHERE WE ARE HAPPY: PLACE

Your Kingdom come

Through this, we are asking God to restore to us the place or country to which we originally belong. Heaven is a place, and it is a kingdom. For His kingdom to come and His will to be done on earth as it is in heaven. When God's will is done in a place, people living there will be happy.

3. GOVERNMENT OF RIGHTEOUSNESS, JUSTICE, TRUTH, AND MERCY: POWER

Your Kingdom come

When God's kingdom comes, His government also comes. We cannot separate His kingdom from government. His kingdom is the government.

4. SIGNIFICANCE: PURPOSE

Your will be done

God's will is His purpose. He has a will and plan for each of us. His desire is for His will to be done, not just in our lives, but on the entire planet.

THE KINGDOM PRAYER: KEYS TO MEETING ALL OUR NEEDS

5. FOOD AND SHELTER: PROVISION

Give us this day our daily bread.

Adam's provision was included in the garden. When we discover His kingdom, our provision will be added to us.

6. FULFILLING RELATIONSHIPS: PERSON

And forgive us our debts, as we forgive our debtors.

Forgiveness is the key to an enduring and fulfilling relationship. God decided to forgive our sins and restore us back to Him as His children. Then He asked us to forgive one another. If you have been in any relationship for any period of time, you will realize that unless you are willing to forgive, that relationship won't last long. Through this prayer, Jesus is giving us the key to fulfilling relationships.

7. SAFETY: PROTECTION

And do not lead us into temptation, but deliver us from the evil one.

That is protection. We need His protection every moment of our life. Our enemy walks around like a roaring lion to see whom he may devour.

8. HAPPINESS: PLEASURE

For Yours is the kingdom and the power and the glory forever. Amen.

Knowing the King, and knowing the kingdom and the power and the glory that belong to our Father, and having the privilege of living in His kingdom, should give us the greatest pleasure—much more than watching or experiencing any form of entertainment ever could.

In the following lines, I want to explain a little bit more the mysteries hidden in this prayer.

I do not believe we need to pray for His kingdom to come anymore because according to Mark 9:1, the kingdom of God already came with power on the day of Pentecost. Now we need to pray for its manifestation, and administer it to execute the will of God on earth as it is in heaven.

> **In this manner, therefore, pray:**
> **Our Father in heaven,**
> **Hallowed be Your name.**
> **Your kingdom come.**
> **Your will be done**
> **On earth as it is in heaven.**
> **Give us this day our daily bread.**
> **And forgive us our debts,**
> **As we forgive our debtors.**
> **And do not lead us into temptation,**
> **But deliver us from the evil one.**
> **For Yours is the kingdom and the power and the glory**
> **forever. Amen. (Matthew 6:9-13)**

OUR FATHER IN HEAVEN

The prayer starts with "our Father in heaven," not "my Father in heaven." This signifies a community or family, telling us that God has more than one child on this planet. The first thing God wants us to know about prayer is that it is a family business, not a religious duty. We need to keep that in our mind as we learn about His kingdom. Sometimes we get so focused on ourselves that we forget that God has other children. He has a big family.

THE KINGDOM PRAYER: KEYS TO MEETING ALL OUR NEEDS

Even though God is a King, we relate to Him as a Father. Why does God want to relate to us as a Father? Some of the major problems in this world today are fatherlessness and father wounds. Many have grown up without a father figure in their lives or with emotional wounds that were inflicted by their fathers or their father figures. Children are supposed to inherit their identity, value, purpose, and destiny from their father.

One of the main responsibilities of parenting is to represent and reveal God to our children, and then to guide our children to have a personal relationship with Him. God knew the challenges fathers would face and how the enemy would attack them to confuse children about their identity, value, and purpose. He Himself decided to relate to each human being as their Father.

Once we discover our heavenly Father, we discover our true identity, value, purpose, and destiny. The majority of us did not receive from our fathers what we were supposed to receive. Once you accept God as your heavenly Father, He is the only One who has any right to have any opinion about us, and His is the only opinion we should believe.

Another responsibility of a father is to protect, provide, and teach his children. Children look to their fathers to protect them, provide for them, and teach the lessons of life. Most children feel secure and safe when they are with their father or when their father is at home. At least, they are supposed to feel that.

The enemy knew that if he could distort the fathers and wound them, they would not be able to portray God to their children, and the children in turn would never want anything to do with God. It is generally accepted, in both Christian and Therapeutic communities, that most children view God based on the experience they have with their earthly father while growing up.

HALLOWED BE YOUR NAME

After we have a revelation of our Father, the second thing He wants us to know about is His name. He wants His name to be made holy on earth and in our lives. What does holy mean? The holiness of God is a combination of many of His attributes. Holy means pure. God is pure in all of His dealings with us. It also means without any defilement or blemish. His love, faithfulness, and compassion toward us are pure. He wants His name to be made holy in our lives. He wants us to be pure in all of our dealings because we represent Him on earth.

The Bible says that without holiness no man can see God (Hebrews 12:14). Jesus said, "Blessed are the pure in heart, for they shall see God" (Matthew 5:8). Holiness is not an outward expression we obtain by wearing a particular style or color of clothing. Our inner holiness will reflect itself in every aspect of our lives.

What is in His name? Why is God so particular about His name? We know God and His nature and character through His names, which are revealed in His Word. Everything He does toward us or for us is a revelation of one of His names.

Every miracle in the Bible is a manifestation of one of His names. If He provides for you, that provision is the manifestation of His name, Jehovah Jireh. If He heals you, that is a manifestation of His name, Jehovah Rapha. Jesus said in His high priestly prayer in John 17:6, "I have manifested Your name to the men whom You have given Me out of the world."

Jesus also said that whatever we ask the Father in His name, He will do it for us (John 14:13-14; 15:16; 16:23-24, 26). For every need you have, there is a name of God through which you can access the provision He has in His kingdom.

THE KINGDOM PRAYER: KEYS TO MEETING ALL OUR NEEDS

That is why He said when we ask in His (specific) name, He will answer us.

YOUR KINGDOM COME

It is interesting to note that most Christians are waiting to go to heaven, when God's desire and purpose is to bring heaven down to earth—for His kingdom to come on earth. That is His priority. What does it mean to pray for God's kingdom to come? What does it look like, practically? God never intended for our lives to be any different on earth than in heaven. He wants us to have the same quality of life right now. Does everyone experience that? No.

God created man to live in His kingdom. He knows that man cannot survive without it, and He wants to give it to His children. He also wants us to live on earth depending on His kingdom, not on this world. He wants us to influence earth with heaven. The earth is limited; His kingdom is unlimited. Earth is natural; His kingdom is spiritual. We are natural and spiritual at the same time. We are a spirit living in a body.

God is the Creator and original Owner of this planet. He created it to extend His kingdom, but it was taken over by the enemy. He is in the process of reclaiming it. That is why He told us to pray for His kingdom to come once again. We are the only agents through which that vision can materialize. Jesus came and taught us the principles and mysteries of His kingdom and about how to administer and operate it here.

We have not fully gotten hold of God's vision yet. Most of us don't even pray the prayer He taught us to pray. This prayer must be prayed by all of God's children worldwide. Imagine more than a billion saints across the world praying that prayer. Do you know why the Roman Catholic Church has the influence it has? They don't speak (at least most) in tongues and roll on the floor, but they pray that prayer almost every time they meet.

When we pray for His kingdom to come, we are praying for His rule, His system of operation, His dominion to come to earth and to every area of our lives: for His kingdom to come in our personal lives, family, finances, etc.; for kingdom economy to come to our finances; for kingdom family to come to our marriages; for kingdom agriculture to come to our eating habits; and for kingdom culture to come to our way of doing things. Each area of our life needs to come under the influence of His kingdom.

YOUR WILL BE DONE ON EARTH AS IT IS IN HEAVEN

Every king has a will and a plan and wants to see it accomplished in his kingdom. God is a King, and His will is accomplished in heaven, as He wants it to be. But on earth, there has been opposition, and someone else's will is being accomplished instead. Right now, in most parts of the earth, Satan's will is accomplished instead of God's.

Some people say that God's sovereignty rules everywhere. That is partially true. He has the final say on everything, but if that were entirely true, then He would not have told us to pray for His will to be done here as it is in heaven because it would already have been made manifest.

You and I are part of that team to see God's will accomplished on earth as it is in heaven. The church is supposed to be teaching and training people to do that, instead of teaching them to sing. We need to learn what God's will is and how He does it in heaven, and copy that on earth. God has a will and plan for every area of our lives. When we deviate from that, we will encounter enormous problems.

THE KINGDOM PRAYER: KEYS TO MEETING ALL OUR NEEDS

There is no poverty, lack, or sickness in heaven because it is not the King's will to have them in heaven. Those did not originate in heaven. They are the works of the devil. That is why the Bible says the Son of God was manifested to destroy the works of the devil (1 John 3:8).

As I mentioned earlier, God put man in Eden where, originally, His will was done as it was in heaven. Then it was man's task to duplicate, expand, and make the entire earth like Eden: to cause the entire earth to be filled with God's kingdom and glory (Numbers 14:21; Psalm 72:19; Habakkuk 2:14). We failed in that task, and through Jesus He restored that kingdom back to us. Then He gave that assignment to the church: to go and preach the gospel of the kingdom, and to fill the earth with the knowledge of His glory.

The Word of God is the revealed will of God. Whatever the Word says we are, that is what we are, and whatever the Word says we should have, that is what we should have. Whatever the Word says we should do, that is what we should be doing.

GIVE US THIS DAY OUR DAILY BREAD

In a kingdom, it is the king's responsibility to take care of the citizens: to make sure everyone has enough to eat and that they are protected. If a citizen of a kingdom is poor, that affects the reputation of the king. God our King guarantees our daily provision, so we should not be worrying about it. The only thing you and I need to make sure of is that we are citizens of His kingdom.

You could be a member of a church and not be a citizen of God's kingdom.

That is a sad dilemma because most people think that because they go to church on Sunday morning they are automatically citizens of God's kingdom. The first requirement for becoming a citizen of God's kingdom is to become a child of the King. Whatever we need for our daily life is called "bread" in the Bible. There are different kinds of bread. I will mention a few of them.

1. NATURAL FOOD

First, we all need physical bread, or food, every day. God is faithful and is committed to providing that for us. He feeds the birds and animals in the forest, so how much more will He take care of His own children?

> **He causes the grass to grow for the cattle, and vegetation for the service of man, that he may bring forth food from the earth, and wine that makes glad the heart of man, oil to make his face shine, and bread which strengthens man's heart.(Psalm 104:14–15)**

Jesus promised to provide everything we need if we seek His kingdom first. He promised to provide food and all the other basic provisions we need in our lives. If anyone out there is lacking the basics for their lives, that means they are not seeking His kingdom first.

2. HEALING

Healing is called "bread" in the Bible. There are many viruses and sicknesses our body fights each day, keeping us safe from them. If it were not for our immune system, which is God's healing system in our body, we all would have died. We need healing every day of our lives. Jesus called healing "the children's bread":

> **And behold, a woman of Canaan came from that region and cried out to Him, saying, "Have mercy on me, O Lord, Son of David! My daughter is severely demon-possessed." But He answered her not a word. And His disciples came and urged Him, saying, "Send her away, for she cries**

> *out after us." But He answered and said, "I was not sent except to the lost sheep of the house of Israel." Then she came and worshiped Him, saying, "Lord, help me!" But He answered and said, "It is not good to take the children's bread and throw it to the little dogs." And she said, "Yes, Lord, yet even the little dogs eat the crumbs which fall from their masters' table." Then Jesus answered and said to her, "O woman, great is your faith! Let it be to you as you desire."*
> *And her daughter was healed from that very hour. (Matthew 15:22–28)*

3. FINANCIAL BREAD

We need money as long as we live on this earth. Money is also called "bread" in the Bible.

> *Cast your bread upon the waters, for you will find it after many days. (Ecclesiastes 11:1)*

The word "bread" here refers to financial investments.

God is faithful to provide us with the money we need to live. One of the best examples is when Peter wanted to pay the tax. Jesus told him to go and cast the hook, and in the mouth of the first fish would be a piece of money to cover the tax (Mathew 17:27; 2 Corinthians 9:8).

4. EMOTIONAL BREAD

We all have emotional needs, too. Our heavenly Father is faithful to meet our emotional needs. His love, acceptance, and comfort keep our souls emotionally healthy. God is a Shepherd, meeting our physical, emotional, and spiritual needs (Psalm 23; Psalm 51:12).

We need favor, ideas, wisdom, solutions, and guidance. Every day we need to thank God for providing us with our daily bread in all the previously mentioned areas of our lives.

AND FORGIVE US OUR DEBTS AS WE FORGIVE OUR DEBTORS

Everything in God's kingdom flows through relationship. Walking in love and forgiveness is imperative for living in God's kingdom. We are commanded to forgive others as He forgives us. If we do not forgive others, God will not forgive us our sins; it is that important. God forgiving our sins is conditional to us forgiving others.

That sounds a little scary to me. Jesus taught on forgiveness more than once. Some examples are Matthew 18:21–35 and Mark 11:25–26. There will be some people in your life who are hard to forgive. Whenever you pray this prayer, mention their names and release forgiveness from your heart.

AND DO NOT LEAD US INTO TEMPTATION

Every sin originates with a temptation. The enemy is lurking to tempt us every chance he gets. Our great-grandparents, Adam and Eve, were tempted and fell into transgression, and sin entered the world. Jesus was tempted by the enemy, but He overcame it. We are supposed to follow in the footsteps of our Lord and overcome temptations. We are prone to be tempted, and we need the grace of God each day to walk in victory.

The evil one will set snares on our way to trap us in his net. We read in Psalm 91:3:

> **Surely He shall deliver you from the snare of the fowler.**

It is a promise from our heavenly Father to deliver us from those snares.

THE KINGDOM PRAYER: KEYS TO MEETING ALL OUR NEEDS

BUT DELIVER US FROM THE EVIL ONE

The Bible says the enemy is walking around like a roaring lion to find whom he may devour (1 Peter 5:8). We need to ask God daily to deliver us from the evil one, who is Satan, and his works. What are his works? Poverty, debt, curses, sicknesses and diseases, strife, offenses, delays, stealing, fear, deception, and lies are some of his works.

If any of these works are operating in your life, ask the Lord to remove and deliver you from the works of the evil one. He will do it if you ask Him. For the Son of God was manifested to destroy the works of the evil one (1 John 3:8). I have paraphrased the Lord's Prayer below so you can pray it every day before you start your day. If you do, you will notice the difference.

FOR YOURS IS THE KINGDOM AND THE POWER AND THE GLORY FOREVER!

The kingdoms of this world, with their power and glory, belong to our God. The enemy stole that from Him by deceiving man; and when Jesus was tempted, the devil offered Him the world, its kingdoms, and its glory (Luke 4:5–7). Since the enemy took it from us, God wants to restore it through us. That is why Jesus died for our sins. We have been taught that Jesus died to recruit and take a bunch of people to heaven. As the Bible says, sin came through man, and salvation from sin also came through a Man, Jesus Christ (Romans 5:12–17).

If there is any area of your life that is not in alignment with the kingdom of God, you have the right and opportunity now to bring it back into alignment, whether it is your finances, health, family life, children, your community and nation, or anything else. As a kingdom ambassador, this is your responsibility.

DISCOVERING THE LOST KINGDOM

There has been reconciliation between heaven and earth, things in heaven and things on earth, through the blood of Jesus (Ephesians 1:7–10; Colossians 1:19–22). Whenever you see something that is not in alignment with God's will, you need to release kingdom authority by commanding (decreeing and declaring) it back into alignment. I encourage you to pray the Lord's Prayer whenever you can. If you are part of an ekklesia, when you come together, pray this prayer as a group. I have paraphrased the prayer for you below. You are free to personalize it as the Holy Spirit leads you.

Our Father in heaven, hallowed be Your name.
Let Your name be made holy in our nation, in my family, and in the whole earth. Thank You for giving us Your kingdom. Help us to administer it effectively on earth. Teach us how to tap into your kingdom resources to solve problems on this earth.
Let Your kingdom rule and dominion come into my life, family, and nation. Let Your kingdom economy, culture, education, and health come to this earth, in my life, nation, and family.
Your will be done on earth as it is in heaven.
Give us this day our daily, physical, financial, spiritual, and emotional bread.
And forgive us our debts, As we forgive our debtors.
(If there is anyone you need to forgive, say their name and release forgiveness from your heart.)
And do not lead us into temptation, But deliver us from the evil one. Thank You for protecting us from evil, curses, offenses, jealousy, strife, sickness, ignorance, lack, and poverty.
For Yours is the kingdom and the power and the glory forever. Amen.

CHAPTER 11
LIFE IN THE KINGDOM

For the kingdom of God is not eating and drinking, but righteousness and peace and joy in the Holy Spirit.
(Romans 14:17)

How much time did Jesus or the disciples spend doing something to provide for themselves? To my knowledge, none. Jesus was busy doing what His Father sent Him to do, and the provision was included with His work. How did Moses support himself and his family when he was sent to Egypt to deliver the Israelites? His provision was included in the calling.

Jesus was training the disciples to live in His kingdom. After the training, He sent them out to preach. He gave them gifts: the power and authority to heal sicknesses, cast out demons, cleanse the lepers, and raise the dead. When He sent them out, He specifically told them not to take any money or any other provision with them. Why? Because He wanted them to trust Him, and for His kingdom to provide for them.

Remember, your provision is in your purpose. That is the way the work of the kingdom must be done. This revelation will revolutionize how we do ministry and mission work today. Each minister and missionary should receive this revelation before they go out to preach the gospel. It is a truth that needs to be taught.

> ***Provide neither gold nor silver nor copper in your money belts, nor bag for your journey, nor two tunics, nor sandals, nor staffs; for a worker is worthy of his food. (Matthew 10:9–10)***

When they came back from the trip, Jesus asked them if they lacked anything. They said they did not.

> ***And He said to them, "When I sent you without money bag, knapsack, and sandals, did you lack anything?" So they said, "Nothing." (Luke 22:35)***

I heard someone say this would only work in the Jewish culture. That is not true. This will work anywhere in the world. Kingdom principles and culture are universal.

Then, I noticed something very interesting. After Jesus asked them if they lacked anything when He sent them out, and their reply was "nothing," He told them,

> ***But now, he who has a money bag, let him take it, and likewise a knapsack; and he who has no sword, let him sell his garment and buy one. For I say to you that this which is written must still be accomplished in Me: "And He was numbered with the transgressors." For the things concerning Me have an end. (Luke 22:36–37)***

LIFE IN THE KINGDOM

Why would Jesus say something like that? It seems as if He is contradicting Himself. They were still in the Jewish culture. What He was saying was that as long as He was with them, the kingdom was also with them, and their needs would be provided for by the kingdom. He was going to be taken from them for a few days, and they would not enjoy kingdom living for that time period. The kingdom would arrive universally only after His resurrection and ascension—once the Holy Spirit came.

Until then, they would need to support themselves. That's why He told them to take money and other material things. That's also the reason Peter went back to fishing—he had no other means of supporting himself. That's why Jesus did not rebuke Peter for what He did. When the Holy Spirit came and the kingdom of God began to operate on the earth, they never returned to do anything to support themselves, even in the midst of severe persecution or famine. They were in the kingdom of God, and the kingdom of God was within them.

When we are born into His kingdom, every one of His children receives one or more gifts (spiritual and natural). When they develop and use them for His kingdom purpose, they will prosper. Usually, your natural gift will pave or open the way to the place of your purpose.

God will never ask you to do something for Him without ordaining the provision. That is not the kind of God we serve. People all over the world are crying and saying, "God told me to do this, but I don't have the money to do it." That is not the way His kingdom operates. When the king in a kingdom assigns you to do something for him, he will always make sure the provision is made available to you to fulfill that assignment.

THE KINGDOM OF GOD VERSUS OTHER GOVERNMENTS

Regardless of what nation they are in, people are not happy with their government. Failed governments are a universal problem. As Christians, we cannot function without a government, either. Jesus came with a government, which is His kingdom. Men have established different forms of government on earth, but they all failed. When Isaiah prophesied about Jesus, the first thing he prophesied about was a government.

> **For unto us a Child is born, unto us a Son is given; and the government will be upon His shoulder. And His name will be called Wonderful, Counselor, Mighty God, Everlasting Father, Prince of Peace. Of the increase of His government and peace there will be no end, upon the throne of David and over His kingdom, to order it and establish it with judgment and justice from that time forward, even forever. The zeal of the Lord of hosts will perform this. (Isaiah 9:6–7)**

God wants His government (kingdom) to come to this earth and to our lives. In His kingdom, there is no poverty, sickness, curse, unemployment, hunger—no evil thing. Every form of government on this earth promises good things to the people at first, but in the end it oppresses and kills them. That is the goal of every government initiated by the kingdom of darkness.

Earthly governments don't work. It doesn't matter what type it is. People everywhere are blaming their government for all the turmoil and confusion in their countries, whether it is communist China; India, the largest democracy; or the capitalistic society in the United States—all forms of worldly government are failing men. They were never intended to satisfy mankind.

LIFE IN THE KINGDOM

People in every nation are looking for a better government. The only type of government that will satisfy humans is the kingdom of God. When we discover God's kingdom and learn to live in it, we will stop blaming our earthly government.

Jesus said, "The kingdom of God is within you" *(Luke 17:21)*. This means that wherever we go, we carry the most powerful government in the universe inside of us: the kingdom of God, the government of heaven. Most people do not know what to do with it or how to exercise its influence to bring any change to their situations.

Ever since man lost the kingdom of God, the devil began to introduce different forms of government and kingdoms on this earth. The first one was the kingdom of Nimrod in Genesis 10:8–10. He was the first superhero on the earth. His intention was to satisfy the longing of men's hearts. There have been many kingdoms and different forms of government, but none of them solved human problems.

The reason for all the corruption and abuse in this world is that man is not sure how to provide for his basic needs, so people lie, cheat, and steal to accumulate wealth. There is only one solution to all of the corruption—the kingdom of God. When people discover the kingdom, everything they need will be added to them so they will not need to lie, cheat, and steal from others.

That is why Jesus taught about the kingdom more than anything else. It was the most important thing He needed to communicate. Another thing I've noticed is that humans need to be taught everything. Though we are the most intelligent creatures God created, we still need to be taught.

When babies are born, they need to be taught what to eat or not eat, how to walk, how to speak, and basic hygiene. Then around five or six years of age, they go to school and spend the next twelve or more years learning about the world system. What if we spent two years of our life seeking God's kingdom? What would happen to us if we did?

HOW DID I DISCOVER THE KINGDOM OF GOD?

I grew up in a middle-class family in India. My father worked for the government, and my mother stayed home and took care of us. The salary my father received was not enough to cover all the needs at home. Every month, when he received his salary and paid the bills, within three days there was no money left. I remember my mother sending me to my neighbor's houses to borrow rice, sugar, and sometimes money.

I would tell them that we would pay it back when my father got paid the next month. I slept on the concrete floor for eighteen years on a single mat without a mattress. We were three brothers and we longed to have a bicycle. When we were teenagers, our father bought a bicycle that we had to share between the three of us.

It was a requirement in our home to fast twice a week. On Friday and Sunday mornings, there was no breakfast. My mother became sick and passed away when she was fifty-one years old. I began to wonder what was wrong with our spirituality. If we served the Almighty God, why could He not even meet our basic needs?

I grew up in a very religious church. Everything I did was performance based to please God or to buy His acceptance through what I did (without knowing that He already accepted me and was pleased with me because of what Jesus did). I used to clap my hands so hard that it broke the skin and bled, trying to make God happy, not knowing that He was already happy.

Though we had hundreds of churches of all denominations in my small town, not even that town was fully reached with the gospel.

LIFE IN THE KINGDOM

The churches were competing against each other instead of working together to reach the people. The gospel originally reached India through the apostle Thomas, but the nation of India was not impacted by the gospel, even after almost two thousand years.

Most Christians and ministers that I knew were broke and sick, but they all sang and preached about Jesus coming back soon to take us all *home* so *get ready*. It was a pie-in-the-sky or "sweet-by-and-by" gospel they preached. They had nothing to offer for the very real problems the people or nation were facing. I felt there was something wrong with the message we were preaching because it was not working. Jesus did not preach a who-wants-to-go-to-heaven gospel.

In almost every meeting, people were waiting or hoping for God to show up and fix everything in their lives as well as the problems in the world. They also did not realize that Jesus had already come to fix things for us. At the second coming, He is not coming to fix things, but to reign.

Jesus Christ coming in the flesh and walking among men was the greatest manifestation of God on this earth. He came to fix everything that was wrong with humanity. He came to fix the sin problem, which is the root of all the other problems we have. He came to fix the sickness, poverty, and relationship problems. Most people interpreted it as Him coming to take us all to heaven when we die.

The gospel seemed powerless to change anything in the culture or in people's lives. Everybody was hiding behind a religious mask. They claimed they were saved and holy, but they lacked the understanding of what they were saved from. They had no evidence to show of their salvation.

DISCOVERING THE LOST KINGDOM

Then, by the grace of God, I entered into ministry, and pretty soon I was frustrated about that, too, because there were no resources available to do anything God called me to do. The land, and the resources God put in it, are used mostly by the devil and his children.

I was taught that they were not meant for me to use now. I was told that I was created to live in heaven singing for thousands of years. I was not good at singing, so I could not imagine what God would think of my singing to Him for thousands of years. I was disappointed that He did not give me a good singing voice. Maybe He did not love me enough! This is what I thought, and it created even more insecurity in me.

Then I came to the West and saw all its glitter and glamour. Everything is about being successful and having fun. I found the resources I was lacking available in plenty, but behind that fun and success, I saw broken lives and families. I realized the fun and success are really a cover-up, a distraction from what is real. People do not know their purpose. They are not fulfilled, even though they have material abundance.

They are raised to believe the sole purpose of life is to get an education and find a nice job to make some money and have some fun. All the people who had fun by fulfilling the lust of their flesh feel broken and depressed in the latter part of their life.

Almost all of their houses and possessions are owned by banks, so they are enjoying the temporary falsehood of having things without really owning anything. They live and work most of their lives to pay for some pieces of wood and metal. I said to myself: *There is something wrong with this system. There should be something more worth living and dying for.*

The only good thing about me was that I was honest enough in my younger years to admit that what I believed and did was not working for me or for the people I was trying to help. Most people are not honest with themselves because of pride, ignorance, or fear. For some, their religious beliefs blind them, so they live a lie, deceiving themselves and wasting a precious lifetime.

That's when I heard the message of the gospel of the kingdom. It hit me like a bullet, and I knew something had happened in my spirit. All of a sudden, everything the Lord had been teaching me since I was sixteen years old made sense. There was a shift in my being. But it was a seed that had been planted in me. That seed began to germinate and grow day-by-day and year-by-year. Just like Jesus said, the kingdom of heaven is like a mustard seed; though it is one of the smallest of all seeds, when it grows it becomes a very large tree where birds of the sky and animals of the field come to rest *(Matthew 13:31–32)*.

I felt like the man who found the pearl of great price, or the man who found the greatest treasure in a field. I did not know everything about it, but there was an inner satisfaction. I felt like I was home and that I belonged for the first time, and that I had a purpose to fulfill.

For a long time, I was afraid to present what I knew because of the fear of people and because of the religious spirit, so I hid the message of the kingdom for almost fifteen years! I wasn't sure if it was the right message. I also needed to mature in it and know what I was preaching. It had to work for me first before I offered it to others.

The Lord brought my attention back to His kingdom several years ago. In October of 2016, the Lord released me and said it was time to run with His message. I am fully convinced that the message of the kingdom of God is the only message Jesus and the apostles preached, and it is the only message that works to solve the problems this world is facing. When you hear the message of the kingdom, the same thing will happen to you. All of a sudden, you will feel something change inside of you. Things will begin to fall into place and start to make sense. You will find answers to the questions you have been asking all your life.

Be careful with that initial excitement. Don't be like the seed that fell on stony places. Let the seed of the kingdom take root inside of you. Nurture it, develop it, and let your hunger grow. There will be a price to pay to discover the kingdom, just like Jesus shared about the man who found the treasure. Renounce the things and traditions that have no eternal value.

If you stay the course and don't give up, it will only be a matter of time until the seed will grow and begin to bear fruit in your life. If there is no fruit showing up, that means there is something wrong with the root system. Make sure the root is not still stuck in religion and religious belief systems. May the Lord help you navigate the storms and temptations that come when you are transitioning from religion into the kingdom.

HOW IT ALL UNFOLDED

When I was sixteen, God put a desire in my heart, along with my brother and two other friends of ours, to meet and pray. We met once a week at our church building to pray. We prayed from 8:30 in the evening until 4:30 in the morning. We continued to do that week after week. We were not praying for our personal needs. Our prayers were focused on world evangelism.

We prayed for every nation, and we dreamed of God using us in mighty and powerful ways.

Something began to happen in our spirits—God began to put desires in our hearts that weren't there before. Though we couldn't afford to rent a bicycle for an hour for one penny, He began to put desires that had no possibility of happening in the natural.

When God gave us those desires, we wrote them down on paper and prayed over them. We commanded them to manifest in the natural. Sometimes we drew pictures of the things He was showing us. We got so excited that we would run, jump, and shout for joy because of what God showed us in our spirit. Nothing changed in the natural for a long time.

We didn't know we were seeking the kingdom of God. I never heard a message on God's kingdom in our church. God was supernaturally causing us to seek His kingdom. He caused me to discover His kingdom at a very young age. The prayers we prayed then are now being fulfilled in our lives.

Through those prayer meetings, God released His kingdom in my heart. It came in the form of a vision, dream, desire, or passion to do something. God was revealing my calling to me. When you seek His kingdom, your calling will be birthed in your heart, or spirit, by the Holy Spirit, as a picture or desire.

You need to follow the blueprint He shows you. Do not look to the left or right. Everything in the natural will look opposite and impossible to what He has shown you. You need to learn to walk by faith and not by sight.

I stopped living based on my natural circumstances or available resources, and I started to tap into the supernatural unlimited resources of heaven to meet my needs. I began learning how to fulfill the calling He put in my heart. The vision God gave you, and your ability to articulate it in faith, is the channel by which you connect to supernatural (kingdom) resources.

What we began in faith, God has blessed and multiplied. He enabled us to help plant more than 100 churches in six states of India. God has since taken me to more than 50 countries. I have been on the TBN Praise the Lord program a few times. We conducted 17 pastoral conferences and trained more than 10,000 pastors and leaders in 15 countries. We conducted hundreds of crusades and open-air meetings, and established four orphanages in India. We now have an online TV channel called **The Kingdom Network.**

By God's grace, I preached on International Television 8 times and the programs went all over the world. We published 26 books that have blessed thousands of people on six continents. As I write this, I am in an airplane flying to Germany for a conference. I feel the anointing all over me, and I am praying for God to do an extraordinary work in your life as you read this book. We have only begun to do what God has called us to do. It's all because of Him.

During the pandemic, the Lord helped us launch The Kingdom School, and hundreds of students from more than twenty countries went through the training. More than seventy-five percent of the students who took the courses got launched into their kingdom assignment. Now the Kingdom School courses are being taught in more than ten countries by those who have graduated. All the glory belongs to our King, Jesus Christ.

KINGDOM OR SANDWICH FIRST?

If you remove man from the place and purpose God created him, he will go hungry and eventually get sick and die. A man called me after listening to my teaching about the kingdom on our radio program and said, "Brother Abraham, how can this kingdom teaching help a homeless man living under a bridge in downtown Denver? Don't you think he needs a sandwich first before he hears the teaching on the kingdom?" I replied, "The teaching of the kingdom is exactly what he needs! If our heavenly Father feeds millions of creatures every day, imagine the size of His feeding program. So, why do men and women who are created in His image go hungry and die of starvation?"

Jesus did not tell hungry people to seek first a sandwich and then His kingdom. No, He said to first seek His kingdom and then a sandwich will be added as a bonus. The religious spirit has messed us up so much through wrong teaching that we don't even know how to think right. I told this brother the first thing Jesus promised if we seek His kingdom is a sandwich (food and clothing), not heaven.

The real problem is not the hunger problem, nor the homeless problem. The real problem is the fatherless problem. Those homeless people do not know that they have a heavenly Father who loves them and wants to take care of them. Many of us are like the Prodigal Son who left his father's house and stayed in a pigpen like a slave, not even having enough to eat. Whose problem was it, really? Was it because there was no food in his father's house that he was starving?

If he had stayed long enough with the pigs, he would have died. Whose problem was it, his or his father's? It was definitely his. We could not blame the father for his death or his starvation. He was experiencing the consequences of his own choice. He was always welcome to go back to his father's house. We need to find what prompts people to choose to leave their Father's house, and what hinders them from returning to their Father's house.

Thank God the Prodigal Son came to himself and had a revelation. He asked himself how many of his father's hired servants had plenty of food to eat and some left over. And here he was: even though he was a son, he was starving for food. Many people today are like that son. Though God feeds millions of creatures every day, many of His own children live in hunger. That is not His will. Whether a person lives under a bridge or in a palace, the first thing they need to do is seek God's kingdom.

The older brother of the Prodigal Son wasn't any better than a servant, either. Though he was a son and heir of everything his father owned, he never enjoyed or benefited from his father's wealth. Though many are God's children, not very many are benefiting from what their Father owns.

> **Now I say that the heir, as long as he is a child, does not differ at all from a slave, though he is master of all. (Galatians 4:1)**

That is the problem with most of the children of God. We have immense resources that have been made available to us because our Father owns it all, but many of us are struggling to meet our basic needs. That's not right—and it's not the way we should be living. The reason is because we do not understand our purpose.

Following are some of the differences between a good Christian and a kingdom citizen, and how they function.

LIFE IN THE KINGDOM

A Good christian	A kingdom Citizen
Getting saved and going to heaven are the most important goals in life.	Living as a child of God to make a difference on this earth for Him is the most important goal in life.
Christians live singing that we don't belong here: "When we all get to heaven…" or "This world is not my home…"	A kingdom citizen lives like their Daddy owns the planet.
A good Christian pays tithes and gives alms.	Kingdom citizens create wealth for kingdom purposes.
Christians live to study and find a job to make a living.	Kingdom citizens discover their purpose, calling, and gifts, and fulfill it.
Christians live to be good and faithful members of a church.	Kingdom citizens live to execute the will of their heavenly Father.
Christians believe their primary purpose for living is to sing (worship) to God.	A Kingdom citizen's primary purpose is to see God's will done on earth as it is in heaven.
Christians live to see another miracle.	Kingdom citizens live to study and learn God's ways.
For Christians, Sunday morning is the most spiritual day.	For a Kingdom citizen, every day is a spiritual day: "This is the day the Lord has made; we will rejoice and be glad in it." (Psalm 118:24)
Christians live to feel the presence of God.	Kingdom citizens carry and release the presence of God wherever they go.
Christians love their own kind.	Kingdom citizens love everyone.

DISCOVERING THE LOST KINGDOM

The kingdom of God belongs to God, and He wants to give it to His children. Jesus said, "Do not fear, little flock, for it is your Father's good pleasure to give you the kingdom" *(Luke 12:32)*. God wants His children to dwell in His kingdom. God gave the authority to become a child of God to those who believe in Jesus and receive forgiveness of sins.

It will require an enormous amount of wisdom, power, and resources to see God's will accomplished on earth as it is in heaven. Everywhere I go, I hear believers say they wish they had more money to help the kingdom, to start schools, to help ministries and churches, etc. They have a vision from God but lack the resources to fulfill it. The reason they say such things is because of a lack of understanding about their specific calling.

God never intended for us to depend on our limited resources, jobs, wisdom, and power to establish His kingdom on earth. It would not be justice on God's part to ask us to do something of which we are not capable. He knows we are limited without Him, and the resources we have are also limited. That is why He put the *unlimited* kingdom inside of us. Everything His kingdom has is unlimited. His wisdom, power, wealth, and resources have no limit!

Every time we see a need, instead of looking at the limited resources we have, He wants us to learn to tap into His unlimited resources and release them to meet that need—releasing heaven's resources to meet earthly needs. This is the way each child of God is supposed to operate. That is why Jesus told us to seek His kingdom first and that all things are possible to those who believe *(Mark 9:23)*. Believe what? Believe that the kingdom of God is inside of us, and the King has made all of His unlimited resources available to us to see His will done on earth as it is in heaven.

LIFE IN THE KINGDOM

Right now, the Holy Spirit wants you to take off every limit that you (or others) have put on yourself. From the time we are born, we are brought up hearing statements like, "You can't have that," "You can't buy that," "That's too expensive," "That's not for now," "You are stupid," and "You can't do anything right." The kingdom of darkness has programmed our minds with lies. We need to tear down those strongholds and replace them with a kingdom mindset. God speaks truth into us, truth we desperately need to believe and act upon.

HOW DO WE KNOW IF WE ARE LIVING IN GOD'S KINGDOM?

1. DID WE SEE THE KINGDOM WHEN WE WERE BORN AGAIN?

There are millions of believers who are saved and waiting to go to heaven but have no clue about what God has called or created them to do—why He sent them to this earth. They were not taught right about what happened to them when they were born again. According to Jesus, when we are born again, we are supposed to see the kingdom of God.

2. IS OUR IDENTITY AS SONS AND DAUGHTERS RESTORED?

The first "right" God restores to a person when they believe in Jesus is the right to become a child of God. Are we walking in our identity as sons and daughters of God? If not, we are not living in His kingdom. The kingdom is for the sons and daughters. When our identity is secured, as sons and daughters, the Father will release us to fulfill His assignment. Our assignment has the power to attract resources to us, both spiritual and natural. Until our identity is secured, the Father won't release us to do His assignment. This I how you live a kingdom life in this day and age.

3. IS OUR ASSIGNMENT RELEASED?

Do you know the assignment the Father had in store for you when He released you to the earth? You were designed and created for a specific task to accomplish for His kingdom.

4. IS KINGDOM PROVISION COMING TO YOU?

To fulfill that assignment, the Father had prepared everything you need in your life before you arrived here, just like He did for Adam in the beginning. This is how you know if you are living in God's kingdom or still on your own trying to survive. May the Lord help you to live in and manifest His kingdom on the earth, and be a part of discipling your nation with the gospel of the kingdom.

PRAYER

Dear heavenly Father, thank You so much for giving me Your kingdom and creating me as a king on this earth. Open my eyes to see and receive the mysteries of Your kingdom. Please make me a part of what You are doing on this earth right now. I dedicate my life and everything I have to establishing Your kingdom for Your purpose, to see Your will done on earth as it is in heaven. In Jesus Christ's holy name, I pray. Amen.

> *I believe this book has been a blessing to you. Please use it for Bible study groups. We invite you to email us with any questions you may have about this book. Please feel free to share it with others. This is only an introduction to the subject of the kingdom of God. I could only mention a fraction of the revelation God gave me about His kingdom here. I strongly encourage you to get the remaining volumes in the Discipling Nations series listed on the next page. Join one of the online Kingdom School Courses we offer to discover your purpose, calling, and gifts. To sign up for a free course, please visit www.TheKingdomUniversity.org*

LIST OF OTHER BOOKS & RESOURCES

Discipling Nations Series:

Kingdom Mandate (for any donation)
Discovering the Lost Kingdom (Volume 1) $14.00
Purpose, Calling, and Gifts (Volume 2) $15.00
God's Original Design (Volume 3) $20.00
Seeing, Entering, and Manifesting the Kingdom of God (Volume 4)$20.00
The Ekklesia (Volume 5) $30.00
The Gospel of the Kingdom (Volume 6) $20.00
Power and Authority of the Church (Volume 7) $15.00
Kingdom Family (Volume 8) $15.00
The Birthing of a kingdom nation (Volume 9) $20.00
What Happened to God? (Volume 10) $20.00
7 Dimensions and Operations of the Kingdom of God (Volume 11)$15.00
Kingdom Economy (Volume 12) $15.00
Kingdom Government (Volume 13) $15.00
Releasing Kings and Queens to their Original Intent (Volume 14) $10.00
Kingdom Secrets to Restoring Nations Back to God (Volume 15) $20.00
Keys to Fulfilling Your Kingdom Assignment (Volume 16) $15.00

Kingdom Living Series:

The Three Most Important Decisions of Your Life $15.00
Recognizing God's Timing for Your Life $12.00
Overcoming the Spirit of Poverty $10.00
Seven Kinds of Believers $10.00
7 Dimensions of God's Glory $5.00
7 Dimensions of God's Grace $10.00
7 Kinds of Faith $7.00

Kingdom Books for Kids:

Genesis126 Three Volume Book set for boys $25.00

To place an order:

www.TheKingdomNetwork.org
Phone: 1-800-558-5020
Email: info@TheKingdomNetwork.org

Are you struggling to discover your **PURPOSE ?**
You are not supposed to fit in but stand out !

Sign up today for the upcoming
FREE Online Kingdom Course

DISCOVERING
THE LOST KINGDOM

In this course you'll DISCOVER:

>> Your true identity and purpose
>> What God is doing on the earth and how you can partner with Him in it
>> Why God created the earth and put us on this planet
   And much more ...

Why are people becoming more and more disinterested in **church and religion** globally?
Join the course, and discover **what your soul has been searching for all along.**

FREE BOOK AND STUDY GUIDE

other courses available
>> DISCOVERING PURPOSE, CALLING AND GIFTS
>> SEEING, ENTERING AND MANIFESTING THE KINGDOM
>> GOD'S ORIGINAL DESIGN | FEBRUARY 2024
>> The Ekklesia
>> The Next move of GOD
   And more ...

Register Now @ **www.TheKingdomUniversity.org**

Welcome to

KINGDOM DELIVERANCE
— WORKSHOP —

Are you tired of waiting and looking for breakthroughs? Kingdom of God has the answer.

This kingdom deconstruct workshop is divided into EIGHT major categories which deal with the seven major areas of our life. Each one is connected to the next, and so if one of these areas dysfunctions, it will affect all other areas of your life.

1. Relationship with the Father
2. Spiritual Healing
3. Emotional Healing
4. Recognizing Purpose and Calling
5. Identifying and Mastering Natural and Spiritual Gifts
6. Finances—Learning to Live in Kingdom Economy
7. Healing Relationships
8. Physical Health

Take action now. Order all 8 workshop manuals today !

Thank you so much for taking the courses from The Kingdom University. Taking a course is only the first step. We are pleased to present you with the next step—that of going through the process to get rid of all the extra weights that have been slowing and hindering you from fully living out your kingdom assignment.

Call 1 800 558 5020   www.TheKingdomNetwork.org

www.ingramcontent.com/pod-product-compliance
Lightning Source LLC
Chambersburg PA
CBHW070137080526
44586CB00015B/1737